About Richard Webster

Author of over seventy-five books, Richard Webster is one of New Zealand's most prolific authors. His best-selling books include *Spirit Guides & Angel Guardians* and *Creative Visualization for Beginners*, and he is also the author of *Soul Mates, Is Your Pet Psychic?, Practical Guide to Past-Life Memories, Astral Travel for Beginners, Miracles*, and the four-book series on Archangels, *Michael, Gabriel, Raphael*, and *Uriel*.

A noted psychic, Richard is a member of the National Guild of Hypnotherapists (USA), the Association of Professional Hypnotherapists and Parapsychologists (UK), the International Registry of Professional Hypnotherapists (Canada), and the Psychotherapy and Hypnotherapy Institute of New Zealand. When not touring, he resides in New Zealand with his wife and family.

To Write to the Author

If you wish to contact the author or would like more information about this book, please write to the author in care of Llewellyn Worldwide and we will forward your request. Both the author and publisher appreciate hearing from you and learning of your enjoyment of this book and how it has helped you. Llewellyn Worldwide cannot guarantee that every letter written to the author can be answered, but all will be forwarded. Please write to:

Richard Webster
℅ Llewellyn Worldwide
2143 Wooddale Drive
Woodbury, MN 55125-2989

Please enclose a self-addressed stamped envelope for a reply,
or $1.00 to cover costs. If outside the U.S.A., enclose an
international postal reply coupon.

Many of Llewellyn's authors have websites with additional information and resources. For more information, please visit our website at http://www.llewellyn.com.

ENCYCLOPEDIA
of
ANGELS

RICHARD
WEBSTER

Llewellyn Publications
Woodbury, Minnesota

First Edition
Fourth Printing, 2011

Book design by Steffani Sawyer
Cover art © 2009 by Bridgeman Art Library, London, SuperStock
Cover design by Lisa Novak
Editing by Nicole Edman
Llewellyn is a registered trademark of Llewellyn Worldwide, Ltd.

All biblical quotations herein are taken from the King James Version.

Library of Congress Cataloging-in-Publication Data
Webster, Richard, 1946-
  Encyclopedia of angels / by Richard Webster. — 1st ed.
     p. cm.
  Includes bibliographical references and index.
  ISBN 978-0-7387-1462-2
  1. Angels—Encyclopedias. I. Title.
  BL477.W425 2009
  202'.1503—dc22
                                        2008029308

Llewellyn Publications
A Division of Llewellyn Worldwide Ltd.
2143 Wooddale Drive
Woodbury, Minnesota 55125-2989
www.llewellyn.com

Printed in the United States of America

Other Books by Richard Webster

Contents

Introduction

My maternal grandmother was a rather forbidding woman. One of her major tasks in life was to improve the behavior of her grandchildren. Whenever we did something wrong, even something as simple as picking up the wrong implement to eat with, she would say: "People who are nice to know always know which fork to use." Breaches of etiquette were a horrendous sin. To this day, I can hear her saying, "People who are nice to know…" followed by whatever it was we children were supposed to do. Fortunately, I can also recall some of her more tender moments. She enjoyed sitting on my bed at night, teaching me children's prayers and traditional rhymes, such as:

> Matthew, Mark, Luke and John,
> Bless the bed that I lie on.
> Four angels to my bed,
> Four angels round my head,
> One to watch, and one to pray,
> And two to bear my soul away.

The last line of this poem must have prevented many children from falling asleep, but I didn't think much about the meaning of the words until many years later.

As I was five or six years old when I learned this rhyme, this must have been the first time I heard about angels. The only thing I learned about angels at school was they were "God's helpers." Catholic friends who lived nearby occasionally talked about angels, especially their guardian angels. I remember embarrassing the chaplain at school by asking him a question about guardian angels. He told me that people who went to the school down the road (the Catholic school) had guardian angels, but we didn't need them. I thought this was unfair but didn't know enough about angels at the time to question him further. It was not until I was in my mid-twenties that I discovered that I not only had a guardian angel, but that I also definitely needed him. This book is the result of the fascination I've had with angels since then.

Angels are spiritual beings of light. The word *angel* comes from the Greek word *angelos*, which means "winged messenger." This is because one of their main functions is to carry messages between mankind and God. They also serve and worship God.

The concept of angels is an ancient one. Many early religions believed in beings that could freely travel between this world and the realm of the gods. Jewish legends tell us angels were created on the second day of Creation.

The oldest known illustration of an angel can be found on a six-thousand-year-old stele from Ur. This shows a winged fig-ure pouring the water of life into a cup held by a king. There are many other early examples of winged figures. The enormous part-human, part-animal winged griffins from Mesopotamia are one example. In Assyria, the griffins were considered Cherubim. They were strange figures with human or lion faces and the bodies of bulls, eagles, or sphinxes. These figures show the close relation-ship astrology has always had with angels, as griffins contain the four signs of the zodiac that mark the solstices and equinoxes: Taurus the Bull (spring equinox), Leo the Lion (summer solstice), the Eagle for Scorpio (autumn equinox), and the Water Carrier for Aquarius (winter solstice).

The Egyptian goddess Nepthys was often depicted as a winged figure. The ancient Egyptians believed everyone had an invisible double, called a *ka*. The ka was probably the person's soul, but it may well have been an early form of guardian angel.

Although wings are the most recognized attribute of angels, angels do not necessarily have wings. In fact, until the time of Emperor Constantine, wings were not usually visible when angels appeared. Medieval and Renaissance artists used wings in their paintings to symbolize the spiritual power of angels, as well as their ability to move between Heaven and earth instantaneously.

Zoroaster (sixth century BCE), the Persian prophet, established a religion called Zoroastrianism, which is still practiced today by two or three hundred thousand people in Iran and western India. It is the oldest existing revealed religion. There are three classes of angels in Zoroastrianism: Amesha Spentas ("Beneficent Immortals"), fravashis ("guardian angels"), and yazatas ("angels"). Even these angels were not the first "true" angels. Zoroaster adopted a variety of existing deities, including the *sukali* who were angels for earlier gods.

The influence of the Zoroastrian angels cannot be overemphasized. The angels of Judaism were based on the cosmology established by Zoroaster. Christianity later adopted its angels from the Hebrew tradition. Both the Hebrew and Christian angels had an influence on the angelology of Islam. Although there are major differences in how these religions view angels, they all accept angels as an important part of their religious beliefs.

The Jewish Kabbalah is a valuable source of information on angels. It dates back to the first century CE, but the most important texts were written in the twelfth and thirteenth centuries. Among these texts are the Zohar and the Book of Raziel the Angel. According to legend, God taught the Kabbalah to his angels. The angel Raziel taught Adam the Kabbalah to help him find his way back to God. In the Kabbalah, angels are part of the Divine Energies that keep the universe in a state of balance.

Angels appear in many forms in the Bible. Sometimes they appear as human beings (Genesis 18; 32:10–13; Joshua 5:13–15; Judges 13:1–5). In Exodus 3, an angel appeared as a fiery bush. Cherubs were obviously seen as well, as two were depicted on the Ark of the Covenant (Exodus 25). Michael and Gabriel are the only two angels mentioned by name in the Bible. Raphael is mentioned in the Book of Tobit, and Uriel can be found in the First Book of Enoch and 2 Esdras. Tobit and 2 Esdras are both in the

Apocrypha, fifteen books that were excluded from the Protestant Bible.

A large amount of early Christian material was excluded from the Bible. These are known as extracanonical or pseudepigraphical writings. Examples of these include the Gospel of Barnabas, the Apocalypse of Abraham, the Apocalypse of Paul, the Book of Adam and Eve, the Book of Jubilees, and the Gospel of Peter. At least forty apocryphal gospels were excluded. These books contain a great deal of information on angels and are frequently referenced in this encyclopedia.

By far the most important of the apocryphal books for anyone interested in angels are the three books of Enoch (c. second century BCE). These are the largest source of information on Christian angels, especially the fallen angels. Although the books of Enoch were excluded from the Bible, many of his ideas and stories were included. The parable of the sheep rescued by the good shepherds in the Gospel According to John, for instance, was originally included in the writings of Enoch. Madam Helena Blavatsky, founder of the Theosophical Society, claimed that the Revelation of St. John the Divine was a "grand but reedited version of the Book of Enoch" (H. P. Blavatsky, *The Secret Doctrine*, Volume IV, 65).

Another important source for angelologists is *The Celestial Hierarchy* by Dionysius the Areopagite, written in the late fifth or early sixth century. This anonymous writer created the best-known hierarchy of angels. In the thirteenth century, St. Thomas Aquinas (1225–1274) used Dionysius' hierarchy in his *Summa Theologiae* (1266–1273), still an important book in the Catholic Church. St. Thomas Aquinas considered angels to be "pure intellect." During his lifetime, angels were part of people's everyday lives. Angelology was a compulsory subject in the theological curriculum at the University of Paris, and scholars such as Giovanni Bonaventure (the Seraphic Doctor) and Thomas Aquinas (the Angelic Doctor) created a huge amount of material to slake students' thirst for knowledge.

The medieval grimoires contain a wealth of information on angels and demons. These magic books are largely concerned with methods magicians use to summon angels and demons. *The Lemegeton* (also known as *The Lesser Key of Solomon*) is one of the most famous of these grimoires. The *Goetia*, the first of the five books that comprise *The Lemegeton*, deals largely with seventy-two demons, or evil spirits. The *Theurgia-Goetia*, the second book, deals with a variety of different spirits. The final three books are concerned with angels and good spirits. Johannes Trithemius, Cornelius Agrippa, Peter de Abano, and Dr. John Dee are just a few of the magicians who valued the material in the grimoires and apparently made good use of them.

Dr. John Dee (1527–1608), the best-known magician of the Elizabethan era, and his scryer, Edward Kelley, communicated with angels on an almost daily basis, and kept detailed records of every communication. John Dee's *Spiritual Diaries* are a remarkable record of these encounters.

Emmanuel Swedenborg (1688–1772), the Swedish scientist and mystic, also communicated with angels regularly and wrote many books about his experiences with them. He was able to not only see and talk with angels, but could also travel freely through Heaven and Hell. Swedenborg believed that every angel had lived on earth as a human being before becoming an angel. He wrote many books on his experiences with angels, including *Heaven and Hell* and the eight-volume *Arcana Coelestia*. Swedenborg greatly influenced later thinkers, including Ralph Waldo Emerson and William Blake.

William Blake (1757–1827), the English artist and poet, saw angels throughout his life. When he was nine years old, he saw a tree covered with angels on Peckham Rye, South London. Robert Blake, William's younger brother, died when William Blake was twenty-nine. He saw his brother's spirit leaving the body and reported that Robert's spirit clapped hands with joy and excitement as it rose toward Heaven. William Blake continued to receive angelic visions for the rest of his life.

Blake recorded a fascinating story about angelic contact in his diary. He had been commissioned to illustrate a book and was struggling to draw an angel. In frustration, he asked out loud, "Who can paint an angel?" Instantly, he heard a reply: "Michelangelo could."

"How do you know?" Blake asked.

"I know, for I sat for him. I am the Archangel Gabriel."

Blake was intrigued, but not totally convinced. He suggested the voice might be that of an evil spirit.

"Can an evil spirit do this?" the voice replied.

A bright shape with large wings materialized in Blake's studio. It radiated pure light. The angel grew larger and larger, and finally the roof to Blake's studio opened up and Gabriel ascended to Heaven. According to Blake's diary, Gabriel then "moved the universe." Unfortunately, he didn't clarify this statement, but he did write that he was convinced he had seen Archangel Gabriel.

Rudolf Steiner (1861–1925), the Austrian philosopher and founder of the Anthroposophical Society, was another visionary. He started communicating with angels telepathically at the age of eight. In adulthood, he developed his own cosmology of angels and had a close connection with the Archangel Michael. Rudolf Steiner taught that we are all guided and protected by a guardian angel. This angel has a profound influence on us while we're young but withdraws during adulthood to enable us to learn through our mistakes.

Geoffrey Hodson (1886–1983), a leading Theosophist and clairvoyant, was contacted by an angel called Bethelda in 1924. The information he learned from these meetings became the subject of five books. I was fortunate enough to grow up in the city Geoffrey Hodson lived in, and I heard many of his lectures on angels.

Angels declined in popularity during the Age of Enlightenment in the eighteenth century. This is not surprising, as people started demanding scientific proof about matters that had previously been accepted on faith.

Even as recently as sixty years ago, angels were considered an anachronism. In 1943, the American philosopher Mortimer Adler was asked to contribute an article to a book on the great ideas of Western civilization. The editorial panel was "flabbergasted" when Adler suggested he write an article on angels, and they asked him to write on something else. Adler insisted, and his article duly appeared. This article and the book *The Angels and Us*, which he wrote some thirty years later, heralded the enormous popularity of angels today.

The angels appear to have noticed it, too. Angelic encounters are more numerous today than ever before. The number of books, DVDs, classes, and workshops available on communicating with angels reveals the dramatic increase of interest in the subject. The New Age movement of the twentieth century has created new interest in angels, and today more people than ever are regularly communicating with the angelic kingdom.

How Many Angels Are There?

I thought I was reasonably knowledgeable about angels before starting work on this book. However, I was forced to change my mind when I began researching the subject and discovered how many angels had been named over the years. Trying to unearth information about many of them was a frustrating, but always fascinating, task.

How many angels are there? The logical answer is, "as many as necessary." However, people have never been satisfied with that answer. The prophet Daniel had a vision in which one hundred million angels appeared: "a thousand thousands ministered unto him, and ten thousand times ten thousand stood before him" (Daniel 7:10). The prophet Enoch visited Heaven and saw "angels innumerable, thousands of thousands, and myriads and myriads." The Zohar says six hundred million angels were created on the second day of Creation. It then goes on to say additional angels were created on other occasions. Discussion on the numbers of angels there were in Heaven reached its height in medieval times.

Albert the Great, a Dominican monk and teacher of St. Thomas Aquinas, wrote that each of the nine choirs of angels had 66,666 legions, and each of these had 6,666 angels, making a grand total of almost 4,000,000,000—four billion! Other scholars of the day came up with a much more modest figure: 301,655,722. I still think the answer to the question is, "as many as necessary."

I've included in this book all the angels that are relevant today, no matter what your interest in angels may be. All the major Christian, Islamic, Judaic, and Zoroastrian angels are here, for instance, as are all the main angels invoked by magicians. However, I also deliberately excluded a number of angels for a variety of reasons. The Enochian angels are a highly specialized and complex group. Because it would involve doubling the size of this book to cover them all, they are better served in books on Enochian magic. Consequently, I have included only a few of the more important angels in Dr. Dee's system.

Many angels are known solely by their names. I have excluded them also, as there seemed little point in including thousands of names with no other information. I also excluded most of the angels who probably never existed. These were created by people who thought of suitable names and added "el" to turn them into angels.

Most people will probably use this book for reference purposes, but I hope others will enjoy browsing through it and reading the entries that appeal to them. I hope you enjoy this book and receive both knowledge and pleasure from it.

Abaddon (Abadon, Abbadon, Appolion, or Appolyon): Abaddon is God's destroyer angel and is called a king in Revelation 9:11: "And they had a king over them, which is the angel of the bottomless pit, whose name in the Hebrew tongue is Abaddon." Because of this, Abaddon is also thought to be the angel mentioned in Revelation 20:1–3: "And I saw an angel come down from Heaven, having the key of the bottomless pit and a great chain in his hand. And he laid hold on the dragon, that old serpent, which is the devil, and Satan, and bound him a thousand years, and cast him into the bottomless pit, and shut him up, and set a seal upon him, that he should deceive the nations no more."

Abaddon is also mentioned by name in the Dead Sea Scrolls. See *devil, dragon, Satan.*

Abadiel: See *Abdiel.*

Aban (Aredvi Sura Anahita): Aban is a female yazata angel in Zoro-astrianism. She lives in the starry regions of the sky and looks after the month of October.

See *yazata, Zoroastrianism.*

Abariel: Abariel is mentioned in *The Key of Solomon* as one of the regents of the moon. Because of this, Abariel is often invoked in rituals involving emotions, fertility, childbirth, and female mys-teries. Abariel also protects people from any mishaps involving water. Abariel is a feminine-looking angel. He wears yellow robes with a blue belt. Around his neck is a heart-shaped locket.

Abathar Muzania (Ab-at-ar Muz-an-iah)**:** Abathar Muzania is the angel who weighs the souls of the dead in the cosmology of the Mandaeans, a Gnostic sect which was most influential in the first and second centuries CE. Abathar Muzania is always depicted with a set of scales.

Abdiel (Abadiel): "Servant of God." During the war in Heaven, Abdiel refused to rebel against God, and argued with Satan, saying that Satan had to be weaker than God because God had created him. According to John Milton's *Paradise Lost*, Abdiel flew away, leaving Satan and his supporters behind. He later fought against Satan's forces, and even struck Satan with his sword. Abdiel's fighting skills were commemorated in World War II. Six Abdiel-class minelayers were named after the angel, and they played a valuable role in the war effort. Three of Britain's Royal Navy ships have also been called HMS *Abdiel*. The first of these was launched in 1915. You can call on Abdiel in any matters concerning faith in yourself and faith in God.

See *Satan, war in Heaven.*

Abdizuel (Abdizriel): Abdizuel is one of the twenty-eight angels who govern the mansions of the moon. Abdizuel is responsible for Alzarpha, the twelfth mansion. Abdizuel helps harvests and plantations to prosper and encourages self-improvement. However, he hinders sailors.

See *mansions of the moon.*

Abezethibou (Abezithibod): According to the *Testament of Solomon,* Abezethibou was originally an angel but is now a one-winged demon in Hell. He is believed to have secretly advised Pharaoh to decline when Moses asked him to let his people go. As this ultimately failed, he helped Pharaoh's magicians create magic with the intention of harming Moses, and encouraged the Egyptians to chase the Israelites after they had been allowed to leave Egypt. According to Jewish legend, Abezethibou drowned with the Egyptians in the Red Sea and is still imprisoned under a pillar at the bottom of the sea.

See *demon.*

Abraxas: Abraxas was originally considered the supreme being in Gnosticism. However, as the Gnostic cosmology evolved, Abraxas became a go-between between God and mankind. Abraxas is considered to be the creator of the Aeons. He rules the 365 Heavens.

See *aeons.*

Abrinael (Abrunael): Abrinael is one of the twenty-eight angels who govern the mansions of the moon. Abrinael is in charge of Sadabath, the twenty-fourth mansion. He helps married couples and supports soldiers; he hinders governments.

See *mansions of the moon.*

Abuliel: Abuliel is one of several angels who specialize in carrying prayers to the Throne of God. The others are Akatriel, Metatron, Michael, Raphael, Sandalphon, and Sizouse. Any of these angels can be invoked if you are sending a desperate prayer for help.

See *Akatriel, Metatron, Michael, Raphael, Sandalphon, Sizouse, Throne of God.*

Abuzohar: Abuzohar is one of the angels who look after the moon. Abuzohar is sometimes invoked in ritual magic when matters concerning the moon are involved.

Achaiah (Ay-kar-hee-yah) (**Achajah**): Achaiah is one of the seventy-two Schemhamphoras, a group of angels who bear the various names of God found in Jewish scriptures. In the Kaballah, Achaiah is said to be one of the eight Seraphim. He also acts as guardian angel to people born between April 21 and 25. Achaiah helps people become more patient and accepting. He enjoys researching the mysteries of the universe and uncovering long lost secrets. Achaiah is usually depicted sitting at a desk, studying an ancient manuscript. He has a lined face, appears to be in late middle age, and wears white robes, a red belt, and leather sandals.

See *guardian angels, Schemhamphoras, Seraphim.*

Acrabiel: Acrabiel is one of the ruling angels of the zodiac and is responsible for the sign of Scorpio.

See *zodiac (angels of the).*

Adam: Adam is best known as the first human. However, in the apocryphal Book of Adam and Eve, he is called "the bright angel." In the Second Book of Enoch, he is called "the second angel." The account in the Apocalypse of Moses says Michael took Adam to Heaven in a fiery chariot. The Secret Book According to John claims that Adam was created by a multitude of angels, each responsible for a small part of his body. Krima, for instance, created Adam's fingernails, and Agromauma, his heart. Once he was created, other angels activated him and brought him to life.

See *Michael.*

Adimus: Before 745 CE, Adimus was venerated by the Catholic Church. However, in that year, Pope Zachary, at the Council of Rome, demoted several angels because they were not mentioned by name in the Bible. These angels, known as reprobated angels, were:

Adimus, Inias, Raguel, Sabaoc, Simiel, Tubuas, and the Archangel Uriel. Apparently, that wasn't the end of Adimus' problems. In 1635, Thomas Heywood published *The Hierarchy of Angels*, and wrote that God had condemned Adimus to eternal damnation.

See *Inias, Raguel, reprobated angels, Sabaoc, Simiel, Tubuas, Uriel*.

Adnachiel (Adnakhiel, Advachiel, or Adernahael): Adnachiel, along with another angel called Phaleg, is in charge of the order of Angels. He is known as the angel of independence and looks after anyone involved in pioneering or adventurous activities. He is the Archangel who looks after Sagittarians and the month of November. Adnachiel is tall and athletic. He wears green and brown robes and carries a large bow and a quiver of arrows. His belt is purple. Attached to a cord around his neck is a talisman of the glyph of Sagittarius.

See *Archangels, Phaleg, zodiac (angels of the)*.

Adriel: "My help is God." Adriel is one of the twenty-eight angels who rule the twenty-eight mansions of the moon. He is responsible for Alchil, the seventeenth mansion. In this role he improves bad fortune and makes love long lasting. He also strengthens buildings and assists sailors.

In the Jewish tradition, Adriel is also one of the angels of death. It is possible that Adriel is also the angel Hadraniel.

See *death (angel of), mansions of the moon, Hadraniel*.

Aeons: In Gnosticism, aeons are a special order of angels who emanated from Abraxas, the Godhead. Each aeon was able to create other aeons, but the divine essence possessed less and less power with each generation. The best-known Aeon is Sophia, sometimes called Pistis Sophia. She is the female symbol of wisdom. Her male equivalent is Dynamis, who symbolizes divine power. It is generally thought there are 365 aeons, although different numbers have been suggested. During the sixth century, their influence declined when Dionysius the Areopagite excluded them from his hierarchy of angels.

See *Abraxas, Dionysius the Areopagite, Dynamis, hierarchy of angels, Sophia.*

Aeshma: In Zoroastrianism, Aeshma is the demon responsible for violence and anger. It is Aeshma who causes aggression to build up in people. Originally, according to Persian legend, Aeshma was one of the seven Amesha Spentas, or Archangels. Gradually, Aeshma was transformed into Zend Aeshmo daeva (the demon Aeshma). He is the most likely inspiration for the demon Asmodeus in the Book of Tobit.

See *Amesha Spentas, Archangels, Asmodeus, demon, Zoroastrianism.*

Af: Af is one of the destroying angels, and, in the Jewish tradition, is an angel of death. Apparently, Af helped Hemah when he tried to swallow Moses and succeeded up to his "circumcised membrum." Af lives in the Seventh Heaven and is immensely tall.

See *death (angel of), destroying angels, Hemah.*

Afriel: Afriel has a special interest in young people and can be invoked in any matters relating to children or teenagers. He is also interested in the well-being of young animals. Afriel promotes a positive attitude and a vision of a better world.

Agiel: Agiel is an angel of Saturn and is sometimes invoked by magicians making Saturnine talismans or working with this particular planet.

Ahriman (Ariman, Aharman, or Dahak): Ahriman is the devil, or evil spirit, in Zoroastrianism. Ahriman was the inspiration for the Jewish, Christian, and Islamic adversary, Satan. Ahriman was originally known as Angra Mainyu. His twin brother is Ormazd.

See *Angra Mainyu, devil, Ormazd, Satan, Zoroastrianism.*

Ahura Mazda (Ohrmazd or Ormazd): Ahura Mazda is the supreme being in Zoroastrianism. He looks after Heaven and earth, and is constantly fighting for the forces of good. His main foe is Angra Mainyu, the devil in Zoroastrianism. Ahura Mazda is helped in his work by six Amesha Spentas, or Beneficent Immortals, who serve as his Archangels. Artists depict him with a long beard, and he usually wears a robe covered with stars.

See *Amesha Spentas, Angra Mainyu, Archangels, devil, Ormazd, Zoroastrianism.*

Ahurani: Ahurani are female yazata angels in Zoroastrianism. Their task is to look after water.

See *yazata, Zoroastrianism.*

Air, Angel of: See *Chassan.*

Airyaman: Airyaman is a yazata angel in Zoroastrianism who is responsible for healing and friendship.

See *yazata, Zoroastrianism.*

Akathrielah Yelod Sabaoth (Ak-ath-reel-yah Yay-lod Sab-ay-ot): Akathrielah Yelod Sabaoth is a powerful angel in Jewish legend. He ranks above all the other angels and stands at the entrance to Heaven.

Akatriel: Akatriel is the angel-prince who proclaims divine mysteries. He is one of the supreme regents of the Seventh Heaven and is a member of the Sarim. Akatriel can be consulted whenever doubt or mystery surrounds a problem.

See *Sarim.*

Aker: According to the Book of Esdras, Aker is one of the nine angels who will govern the world after the Day of Judgment. The others are: Arphugitonos, Beburos, Gabriel, Gabuthelon, Michael, Raphael, Uriel, and Zebuleon.

See individual angels.

Akhazriel (Akraziel): "Herald of God." In Jewish lore, Akhazriel is the angel who delivers God's pronouncements and passes on important messages. It was Akhazriel who, for instance, told Moses that his prayer asking for a longer time on earth would not be granted.

Akhshti (Ak-hesh-tee): Akhshti is a yazata angel in Zoroastrianism. He personifies peace.

See *yazata, Zoroastrianism.*

Akriel: Traditionally, Akriel is the angel of barrenness, called upon for help in cases of infertility. Nowadays, he is called upon for help with all problems associated with sexuality, including conception, sterility, and lack of libido. Akriel is also called upon to aid people suffering from mental illness. He also helps people improve their memories and encourages them to undertake mentally challenging tasks. People who are studying and need to memorize a great deal of material also call upon him. Akriel is sometimes called the angel of intellectual achievement. He wears yellow robes with a wide red belt around his waist. In one hand he holds a large red heart.

Aladiah (Al-ar-dee-yah): Aladiah is one of the seventy-two Schemhamphoras, a group of angels who bear the various names of God found in Jewish scriptures. Aladiah is also guardian angel for people born between May 6 and 10. Aladiah heals people emotionally. In the process, he helps them let go of the past and move on with their lives.

See *guardian angels, Schemhamphoras.*

Alan of Lille: Alan of Lille (c.1114–1202) was called Doctor Universalis because of his erudition and knowledge. He was a philosopher, theologian, historian, naturalist, author, and poet. His work on the hierarchy of angels (*Treatise on the Angelic Hierarchy*) explains the gifts, attributes, functions, and tasks of the various angels. He also examines the "antiangels," spiritual beings who constantly fight against angels and try to undermine their good work. Alan of Lille classified antiangels into a hierarchy called Exordo.

See *Exordo, hierarchy of angels.*

Alheniel: See *Atheniel.*

Amael: Amael is one of the rulers of the choir of Principalities and is considered an angel of hope. Amael enjoys working with people who are developing their psychic skills.

See *Principalities.*

Amasras: Amasras is mentioned in the Book of Enoch. He enjoys helping people who work with the soil, such as gardeners and farmers. He is called upon to increase the potency of magic spells.

See *Enoch (Book of).*

Ambriel: Ambriel is Prince of the Order of Thrones and the ruling angel of May. He is generally considered an Archangel and looks after people born under the sign of Gemini. He can be invoked for any matters involving communication. He also assists people who are seeking new jobs or searching for more opportunities and responsibility. Ambriel has long, blonde hair and wears a jacket of rose-red. His belt is silver. Ambriel also wards off evil and is sometimes depicted with one hand raised in front of him to repel negative energies.

See *Archangels, Thrones, zodiac (angels of the).*

Ameretat: Ameretat is an Amesha Spenta, one of the Archangels in Zoroastrianism. She is considered to be the sister of Haurvatat. Ameretat is the angel of immortality and rules over plants.

See *Amesha Spentas, Archangels, Haurvatat, Zoroastrianism.*

Amesha Spentas: Amesha Spentas are the Beneficent Immortals created by Ahura Mazda, the supreme being in Zoroastrianism. They equate to Archangels in Judaism and Christianity. They are sometimes referred to as Holy Spirits. There are six Amesha Spentas, or "holy immortal ones": Ameretat (Immortality), Asha Vahishta (Spirit of Truth), Haurvatat (Wholeness), Khshathra Vairya (Warrior), Spenta Armaiti (Devotion), and Vohu Manah (Righteous Thinking). Ahura Mazda and the amesha spentas are the Holy Immortals who protected the world when it was first created.

See *Ahura Mazda, Archangels,* individual angels, *Zoroastrianism.*

Amitiel: Amitiel is generally considered the angel of truth. (However, both Gabriel and Michael have also been given this title at times.) He can be called upon for help in any matters requiring honesty and integrity. According to Jewish legend, Amitiel argued against the creation of humanity because he felt humans would ultimately turn against God and cause enormous misery and distress. Amitiel wears white robes and has a large pendant of a cross on his chest. His right hand is held at head height, with the first two fingers upraised. His thumb holds the other two fingers in his palm.

See *Gabriel, Michael.*

Amnediel: Amnediel is one of the twenty-eight angels who govern the mansions of the moon. Amnediel is responsible for Alnaza, the eighth mansion. Amnediel helps create friendship, love, and happy times for travelers. He also repels mice and imprisons captives.

See *mansions of the moon.*

Amnitziel (Amnitzial): Amnitziel is considered to be the Archangel who looks after the astrological sign of Pisces and the month of February. He is assisted by Vakhabiel.

See *Archangels, Vakhabiel.*

Amnixiel: Amnixiel is mentioned in a list of the seven electors in Hell, which, if true, makes him a fallen angel. He is also listed as one of the twenty-eight angels who govern the mansions of the moon. Amnixiel is responsible for Albotham, the twenty-eighth mansion. In this role, he enhances businesses, ensures the safety of travelers, increases the happiness of married couples, and strengthens prisons. Unfortunately, he also causes the loss of treasure.

See *fallen angels, mansions of the moon.*

Amutiel: Amutiel is one of the twenty-eight angels who govern the mansions of the moon. Amutiel is responsible for Allatha, the nineteenth mansion. Amutiel is a negative angel who supports warfare, the creation of refugees, and the death of sailors and prisoners.

See *mansions of the moon.*

Anabiel: According to the Kabbalah, Anabiel can be called upon to cure stupidity.

Anael (A-na-oo-el) **(Anapael, Anapel, Aniel, or Hagiel):** "The Grace of God." Anael is a member of the Sarim, and Chief of both the Order of Principalities and Virtues. He is also a planetary angel, Lord of Venus, and Ruler of the Third Heaven. As a result, he can be invoked for any matters concerning love, romance, affection, sexuality, peace, harmony, and inner peace. Because of his association with love and affection, Anael is usually considered an Archangel and is probably the most frequently invoked angel of all. He is also concerned with long-term careers, status, and recognition. Anael rules the month of December and looks after people born under the sign of Capricorn. He is also guardian angel for people born between September 24 and 28.

According to the Book of Enoch, Anael transported Enoch to Heaven in a fiery chariot. Anael helps people who are engaged in creative pursuits, and he endeavors to create beauty wherever he goes. Anael helps people overcome shyness and gain confidence in themselves. Rudolf Steiner listed Anael as one of the seven great Archangels.

Anael is sometimes mistakenly assumed to be Haniel.

See *Archangels, Enoch (Book of), guardian angels, Haniel, planetary angels, Principalities, Steiner (Rudolf), Sarim, Virtues, zodiac (angels of the)*.

Anafiel (Anaphiel or Anapiel): Anafiel is a member of the Sarim and head of the eight principal angels of the Merkabah. In this role he looks after the keys to the palaces of Heaven. According to the Third Book of Enoch, Anafiel was the angel who carried the prophet Enoch up to Heaven. His importance is indicated by the fact that he whipped the powerful angel Metatron sixty times with tongues of fire after Metatron had transgressed in some way.

See *Merkabah, Metatron, Sarim*.

Anahel: According to the Sixth and Seventh Books of Moses, Anahel is a ruler of the Third Heaven but serves in the Fourth of the Seven Heavens.

See *Heavens*.

Anahita (Anaitis): Anahita is one of the angels of fertility. Anahita can be invoked for help in any matters concerning fertility and pregnancy. Anahita is a female yazata in Zoroastrianism.

See *yazata, Zoroastrianism*.

Anamchara: The anamchairde (plural of anamchara) were guardian angels of the ancient Celts. They have a special interest in people who are developing spiritually but are willing to help anyone when necessary.

See *guardian angels*.

Ananchel: According to Jewish tradition, Ananchel was one of the three angels sent by God to give advice to Esther. At that time, the king of Persia had a disobedient wife called Vashti, and a Jewish virgin named Esther became her replacement. Because of this, Esther was able to prevent a plot to kill all the Jews in Persia.

Archangel Michael was one of the other angels who spoke to her. Ananchel helps people open their hearts to receive God's love.

See *Archangels, Michael.*

Anas: According to a twelfth-century manuscript in the British Museum, Anne, the Virgin Mary's mother, was transformed into an angel called Anas. There are four or five other reported instances of humans becoming angels. By far the best known is the prophet Enoch, who became the great angel Metatron. Jacob apparently became the Archangel Uriel; St. Francis of Assisi became the angel Rahmiel; and the prophet Elijah became Sandalphon. Members of the Church of Latter Day Saints believe the angel Moroni was originally a man of the same name.

See *Angelification, Archangels, Metatron, Moroni, Rahmiel, Sandalphon, Uriel, Virgin Mary.*

Anauel: Anauel is the angel of prosperity and commerce. He looks after people involved in business or financial matters. He can be invoked in any matters concerning money or finance. Anauel is also the guardian angel of people born between January 31 and February 4. Anauel has brown hair and wears green robes. He is usually depicted with a small leather or cloth bag in one hand, which possibly holds gold coins.

See *guardian angels.*

Anaviel: Anaviel is one of the seventy-two Schemhamphoras, a group of angels who bear the various names of God found in Jewish scriptures.

See *Schemhamphoras.*

Angel: The word *angel* is derived from the Greek *angelos*, which means "messenger." Angels are the lowest ranked members of Dionysius the Areopagite's Hierarchy of Angels. Their main tasks are to act as God's messengers and to help individual people in the world. Guardian angels belong to the choir of Angels. Several angels have been said to rule the choir of Angels, including Gabriel, Adnachiel, and Chayyiel.

See *Adnachiel, Chayyiel, Dionysius the Areopagite, Gabriel, guardian angels, hierarchy of angels.*

Angelic Doctor: St. Thomas Aquinas is called the angelic doctor because of his interest in angels and writings on the subject.

See *Aquinas (St. Thomas).*

Angelification: Angelification occurs when a human being is transformed into an angel. The best known instance of this is the prophet Enoch who became the great angel Metatron (3 Enoch: 3). According to tradition, the prophet Elijah became the angelic prince Sandalphon, who is sometimes referred to as Metatron's brother. St. Francis of Assisi (c.1181–1226) is also believed to have become the angel Rahmiel. Jacob became the Archangel Uriel, and the Virgin Mary's mother Anne became the angel Anas. Moroni, the angel who communicated with Joseph Smith and told him where the gold plates containing the Book of Mormon were buried, is believed to have originally been a man also named Moroni.

See *Anas, Archangels, Metatron, Moroni, Rahmiel, Sandalphon, Uriel.*

Angelolatry: Angelolatry is the adoration and worship of angels. For thousands of years, people have debated whether or not it is idolatry to worship angels. In The Revelation of St. John the Divine, an angel stops John from worshiping him: "And I John saw these things, and heard *them*. And when I had heard and seen, I fell down to worship before the feet of the angel which shewed me these things. Then saith he unto me, See *thou do it* not: for I am thy fellowservant, and of thy brethren the prophets, and of them which keep the sayings of this book: worship God" (Revelation 22:8–9).

Angra Mainyu (An-gra Mah-in-yoo) **(Angra Mainya or Ahaitin):** Angra Mainyu is the devil, or Satan, in Zoroastrianism. He lives in a dark abyss in the far north of the world. He usually manifests himself as a lizard, snake, or young man. Angra Mainyu is believed to have divided human speech into thirty languages, causing problems with communication between peoples. After Ahura Mazda created the stars in Heaven, Angra Mainyu created the planets so their astrological influence would have an effect on everyone. His main foe is Spenta Mainyu. Angra Mainyu gradually evolved and ultimately became Ahriman.

Angra Mainyu had numerous assistants who helped him fulfill his role as Evil Spirit. The main ones were Akoman (Evil Mind), Indra Vayu (Death), Saurva (Death and Disease), and Tauru and Zairi, two demons whose functions are not known. Other demons included Aeshma (Violence and Fury), who may well be Asmodeus, the famous demon in the Book of Tobit; Az (Lust); and Mithandruj (Dishonesty and Lies).

See *Aeshma, Ahriman, Ahura Mazda, Asmodeus, demon, devil, Satan, Spenta Mainyu, Zoroastrianism.*

Aniel (Ah-nee-el): Aniel is one of the seventy-two Schemhamphoras, a group of angels who bear the various names of God found in Jewish scriptures.

See *Haniel, Schemhamphoras.*

Anixiel: Anixiel is one of the twenty-eight angels who govern the mansions of the moon. He is in charge of Alchaomazon, the third mansion. Anixiel helps alchemists, hunters, and sailors.

See *mansions of the moon.*

Annan: In the Islamic tradition, Annan is an angel who helps Thunder look after the clouds.

See *Thunder.*

Annunciation, Angel of the: Gabriel is the angel of the Annunciation. He came to Mary to tell her she was going to give birth to Jesus. The Annunciation has always been a popular subject in religious art, and religious artists frequently depict this moment in their paintings. Gabriel is usually shown with a lily, which is Mary's flower. The biblical account of the Annunciation reads: "And in the sixth month the angel Gabriel was sent from God unto a city of Galilee named Nazareth. To a virgin espoused to a man whose name was Joseph, of the house of David; and the virgin's name *was* Mary. And the angel came in unto her, and said, Hail, *thou that art* highly favoured, the Lord is with thee: blessed *art* thou among women. And when she saw *him*, she was troubled at his saying, and cast in her mind what manner of salutation this should be. And the angel said unto her, Fear not, Mary: for thou hast found favour with God. And, behold, thou shalt conceive in thy womb, and bring forth a son, and shalt call his name Jesus" (Luke 1:26–31).

See *Gabriel, Jesus.*

Anpiel: According to Jewish lore, Anpiel is the angel who is responsible for looking after birds. Anpiel lives in the Sixth Heaven, where one of his tasks is to ensure that prayers arrive safely in Heaven. This association may have occurred because birds are often considered symbols of the spirit, and their ability to fly high in the sky symbolizes prayers flying up to Heaven. Once the prayers arrived in the Sixth Heaven, Anpiel crowned them and sent them on to the Seventh Heaven. Jewish legend says Anpiel escorted Enoch to Heaven.

Anthroposophy: Anthroposophy is a philosophical and spiritual system developed by Rudolf Steiner. The Anthroposophical Society was established in 1912. Steiner based his teachings on Buddhist, Christian, Hindu, Rosicrucian, and Theosophical ideas. He was also influenced by the works of Johann Wolfgang von Goethe (1749–1832). *Anthroposophy* is the term Steiner used to describe his esoteric system to distinguish it from the teaching of the Theosophical Society, which he left in 1913. The word *theosophy* was originally invented by an English mystic, Thomas Vaughan

(1622–1666), who used it in his book *Anthroposophia Theomagica* (1650). The term was used by a number of philosophers in the nineteenth century. One of these was Robert Zimmermann (1824–1898), who taught Rudolf Steiner at the University of Vienna. Steiner believed in reincarnation, karma, the akashic records, and the process of spiritual evolution, in which human beings gradually ascend to higher levels of consciousness. Anthroposophy teaches a series of meditative exercises that enable students to develop their spiritual awareness. The ultimate aim is to reach a state of enhanced consciousness where humans can see the spiritual world. Rudolf Steiner called his system a "spiritual science." Steiner's system also encompasses art, biodynamic farming, color, education, eurythmy, and medicine. The headquarters of the Anthroposophical Society in Dornach, Switzerland, are called the Goetheanum, as a tribute to Goethe and his writings.

See *Steiner (Rudolf)*.

Apocalypse, Angel of the: The angel of the apocalypse will tell humankind that the end of the world is about to occur, and the entire human race will be judged. Different authorities have suggested several possible angels for this task. They include: Michael, Gabriel, Raphael, Haniel (Aniel), and Orifiel.

See individual angels.

Apocrypha: The word *apocrypha* means "things that are hidden." The Apocrypha is part of the Roman Catholic Bible and contains a great deal of information about angels, especially the Books of Esdras and the Book of Tobit. The fifteen books that make up the Apocrypha were probably written between 200 BCE and 200 CE. Most of the early fathers of the Christian church accepted the Apocrypha as it was included in the Septuagint, the Greek version of the Old Testament. However, in the fourth century, St. Jerome compiled his Latin version of the Bible, called the Latin Vulgate. Although he included the Apocrypha, he remarked that they belonged in a separate category of their own. The first English version of the Bible was a translation of the Latin Vulgate. It was published in the late fourteenth century and included all of the Apocrypha except for 2 Esdras. The Protestant Reformation increased discussion on the Apocrypha and they were eventually excluded from the Revised Standard Version. However, in 1546, the Council of Trent declared the Apocrypha part of the Christian canon, and anyone who disagreed with this was declared anathema.

The following books and parts of books are generally considered part of the Apocrypha: 1 Esdras, 2 Esdras, Tobit, Judith, Additions to the Book of Esther, the Wisdom of Solomon, Ecclesiasticus (the Wisdom of Jesus the Son of Sirach), Baruch, the Letter of Jeremiah, the Prayer of Azariah and the Song of the Three Young Men, Susanna, Bel and the Dragon, the Prayer of Manasseh, 1 Maccabees, and 2 Maccabees.

Aquinas, St. Thomas: St. Thomas Aquinas (1225–1274), usually called the angelic doctor, was a scholar, philosopher, theologian, and prolific author. His most famous work, *Summa Theologiae* (1266–1273), includes a large section on angels, as well as his five proofs of the existence of God. In this book, he also elaborated on and confirmed Dionysius' Hierarchy of Angels. St. Thomas Aquinas had a huge influence on the acceptance and belief of angels. He believed angels to be "pure intellect." However, they could obtain temporary physical bodies whenever necessary. St. Thomas Aquinas was canonized by Pope John XXII in 1323, fewer than fifty years after his death.

See *hierarchy of angels.*

Arabot (Araboth): Arabot is the name of the Seventh Heaven. God and his most highly ranked angels live here, including the Seraphim, Cherubim, and the angels of dread, fear, grace, and love. In addition, 496,000 camps of ministering angels live here. This is a huge number of angels, as each camp consists of 496,000 angels. Archangel Michael is the prince in charge of Arabot.

See *Archangels, Cherubim, Michael, Seraphim.*

Aral (Arel): Aral is the angel of fire. The term "angel of fire" has been used to describe a number of angels. According to the Zohar, Archangel Gabriel visited Moses in a flame of fire. In Zoroastrianism, Atar is the angel of fire. Archangel Uriel is sometimes considered the angel of fire because his name means "flame of God." Ardarel is sometimes referred to as the angel of fire, and Aral might be an abbreviation of this.

See *Archangels, Atar, Gabriel, Nuriel, Uriel, Zoroastrianism.*

Arariel (Arael or Ariael): Arariel belongs to the choir of Thrones. As Prince of the Waters, he is responsible for the oceans and is invoked by fishermen who want to increase the size of their catches. He can also cure stupidity.

See *Thrones.*

Aratron (Arathron or Araton): Aratron is one of the seven Olympian spirits who rule over the 196 sections of Heaven. Aratron is responsible for 49 of these. He also looks after the planet Saturn. Aratron governed the world from 550 BCE to 60 BCE.

See *Olympian spirits.*

Archangels: The prefix *arch* means "chief," "principal," or "most important." Consequently, Archangels are amongst the most important angels. They are God's most important messengers. It was Archangel Gabriel, for instance, who was sent to tell Mary she would give birth to Jesus. The First Book of Enoch lists seven Archangels: Gabriel, Michael, Raguel, Raphael, Remiel, Saraqael, and Uriel. Dionysius also listed seven Archangels in his Hierarchy of Angels: Michael, Gabriel, Raphael, Uriel, Chamuel, Zadkiel, and Jophiel. The Book of Revelation also mentions seven Archangels, though other sources list four, six, nine, or twelve. The Koran recognizes four Archangels, but names only two: Djibril (Gabriel) and Michael. (The other two are possibly Israfil and Izrail [Azrael].) Michael, Gabriel, Raphael, and Uriel are the best-known Archangels. Other possible Archangels include:

Adnachiel, Anael, Asmodel, Barchiel, Cambiel, Cassiel, Hamaliel, Khamael, Malkhidael, Metatron, Mizrael, Orifiel, Perpetiel, Raguel, Raziel, Remiel, Sachiel, Sahaqiel, Salaphiel, Samael, Sandalphon, Saraqael, Sariel, Sidriel, Suriel, Tzaphiel, Verchiel, Zachariel, Zadkiel, Zamael, and Zuriel.

See *Enoch (Book of)*, *hierarchy of angels*, individual angels.

Archons: In the Gnostic tradition, archons are a high-ranking choir of angels who have the responsibility of looking after countries and large groups of people. The four main Archangels (Raphael, Michael, Gabriel, and Uriel) are said to belong to the archons. Gnostics believe the archons rule the different Heavens and make it difficult for souls to progress to the Seventh Heaven to see the face of God. Gnostics also have a concept of demon archons, and seven of them correspond with the seven deadly sins of pride, envy, wrath, lust, sloth, avarice (greed), and gluttony.

See *Archangels*, individual angels.

Ardarel: See *Aral*.

Ardifiel (Ardefiel or Ardesiel): Ardifiel is one of the twenty-eight angels who govern the mansions of the moon. Ardifiel is in charge of Algelioche, the tenth mansion. In this role, he strengthens buildings, promotes love and good feelings, and helps oppose enemies.

See *mansions of the moon*.

Ardoustus: Ardoustus helps people who are trying to nurture someone or something. Ardoustus has a special interest in helping mothers to nurture their babies.

Argaman: Argaman is not the name of an angel, but a mnemonic that was used on amulets to represent Uriel, Raphael, Gabriel, Michael, and Nuriel.

See individual angels.

Ariel (Ah-ree-el): "Lion of God." Ariel is one of the seventy-two Schemhamphoras, a group of angels who bear the various names of God found in Jewish scriptures. He is mentioned in the pseudepigraphal Book of Ezra and the Key of Solomon the King. According to some accounts, he helps Raphael heal humans, animals, and plants. In John Milton's *Paradise Lost*, Ariel was called a fallen angel. However, in Thomas Heywood's *Hierarchy of the Blessed Angels* (1635), he is called "Earth's great Lord." In the Kabbalah, he is the angel of the element of fire. Ariel is guardian angel of people born between November 8 and 12. He helps people set goals and achieve their ambitions. Ariel is also one of the ruling angels of the zodiac and is responsible for the sign of Leo.

See *fallen angels, guardian angels, Raphael, Schemhamphoras, zodiac (angels of the)*.

Ariukh: Ariukh and Mariokh are the two angels who watched over the family of Enoch—later to become the great angel Metatron— to protect and preserve them from the impending Flood. Their actions saved Enoch's bloodline and preserved his writings.

See *Mariokh, Metatron*.

Ark of the Covenant: The Ark of the Covenant housed the Ten Commandments and was guarded by either two or four angels. According to the Bible, two Cherubim were carved into the mercy seat of the Ark (Exodus 25:18–20). Tradition says they were Jael and Zarall. The Ark was carried by the Levites during the period the Jewish people spent in the wilderness. King Solomon finally placed the Ark in the Great Temple of Jerusalem.

See *Cherubim, Jael, Zarall*.

Armaita: See *Spenta Armaita*.

Armisael: Armisael is the "angel of the womb." Because of this, he is traditionally invoked in matters relating to labor and childbirth. He is also sometimes invoked to aid conception. Gabriel and

Temeluch help the baby while it is in the womb, but it Armisael who is responsible for the birth process.

See *Gabriel, Temeluch.*

Arphugitonos: According to the Book of Esdras, Arphugitonos is one of the nine angels who will govern the world after the Day of Judgment. The others are: Aker, Beburos, Gabriel, Gabuthelon, Michael, Raphael, Uriel, and Zebuleon.

See individual angels.

Arshtat: Arshtat is a female yazata angel in Zoroastrianism. She personifies honesty and justice.

See *yazata, Zoroastrianism.*

Artiyail: In the Islamic tradition, Artiyail is the angel who helps people overcome anxiety, stress, and depression.

Asaliah (A-sa-lee-yah): Asaliah is a member of the choir of Virtues. In the Kabbalah, he is said to be an angel of justice. Asaliah is one of the seventy-two Schemhamphoras, a group of angels who bear the various names of God found in Jewish scriptures. He is the guardian angel for people born between November 13 and 17. Asaliah is interested in human potential and the power of thought. He helps aid understanding and assimilation of new material.

See *guardian angels, Schemhamphoras, Virtues.*

Asaph: Asaph is the only angel credited with writing part of the Bible. Apparently, he wrote twelve of the Psalms: number 50, and numbers 73–83. As a result of this, God rewarded Asaph by making him chief of the heavenly hosts who endlessly sing God's praises. According to the Zohar, he performs this task only at night. Heman leads the angels in the morning, and Jeduthan looks after the evening.

See *Heman, Jeduthan.*

Asariel: Asariel is one of the planetary angels. He is the ruler of Neptune and has the task of encouraging people to trust their intuition and act upon it. He looks after people who are involved in clairvoyancy and mediumship. He also helps people develop their creative imaginations. Asariel can also be invoked to help heal sick horses.

See *planetary angels.*

Asbeel: Asbeel was one of the leaders of the Grigori. He encouraged the other angels to defile their bodies by sleeping with human women.

See *Grigori.*

Asha Vahishta: Asha Vahishta is one of the seven Amesha Spentas, or Beneficent Immortals, in Zoroastrianism. Asha Vahishta ensures that everything in the universe occurs in the correct, lawful order. He is also responsible for fire, which was sacred to the Zoroastrians. Asha Vahishta offers justice and spiritual knowledge to anyone who asks for it.

See *Amesha Spentas, Zoroastrianism.*

Ashi Vanghuhi: Ashi Vanghuhi is a female yazata angel in Zoroastrianism. She bestows blessings on people who deserve them.

See *yazata, Zoroastrianism.*

Asman: Asman is a yazata angel in Zoroastrianism. He rules over the sky.

See *yazata, Zoroastrianism.*

Asmodel (Ashmodiel): Asmodel governs the month of April and is responsible for people born under the sign of Taurus. He is considered an Archangel. Asmodel is cautious and helps people steadily increase their net worth. He can be invoked on any matters involving love and romance. Asmodel's robes are dark-green and turquoise. He appears relaxed and is usually seen sitting down reading a scroll.

See *Archangels, zodiac (angels of the)*.

Asmodeus: Asmodeus is the demon in the Book of Tobit who was outwitted by the Archangel Raphael, and "banished to upper Egypt." In this story, Tobias marries Sarah, a young woman who has had seven previous husbands. All these marriages were unconsummated, as Asmodeus had killed her husbands on their wedding night to prevent them from making love to her. Raphael told Tobias to make smoke from the gall and heart of a fish, and this drove Asmodeus away.

Asmodeus was originally a Persian spirit who provoked anger and a desire for revenge. In the Jewish tradition, Asmodeus caused marital problems, preventing sexual relations between man and wife and encouraging adultery. Partly because of this, Asmodeus gradually became considered a demon of lust. According to Jewish legend, Asmodeus was the son of a mortal woman called Naamah and a fallen angel. Today, Asmodeus is said to be in charge of all the gambling establishments in Hell.

See *Archangels, demon, fallen angels, Raphael*.

Astanphaeus (Astan-fay-us)**:** In the Gnostic tradition, Astanphaeus was one of the seven Elohim of the Presence. In Jewish lore, he is associated with the planet Mercury.

See *Elohim, Presence (Angels of the)*.

Astrological Angels: Astrologers erect their charts using the sun, moon, and planets. Consequently, they are in a sense dealing with the celestial realms. Early on, people associated the planets with different qualities. Mars, for instance, was associated with war, and Venus with love. Angels were also given a variety of associations. The planetary angels looked after the seven major planets and the days of the week. Other angels looked after rain, wind, thunder, and other weather conditions. The signs of the zodiac were developed some five thousand years ago, and zodiac angels are responsible for them. Eventually, people were assigned their own guardian angels.

See *day (angels of the)*, *guardian angels*, *planetary angels*, *zodiac (angels of the)*.

Asuryal (Arsyalalyur): According to the First Book of Enoch, Asuryal was the angel God sent to Noah to warn him that the Flood was about to commence.

Ataliel (Atliel): Ataliel is one of the twenty-eight angels who govern the mansions of the moon. Ataliel is in charge of Agrapha, the fifteenth mansion. In this role he helps find buried treasure but also creates discord, divorce, and the destruction of houses and enemies. He also hinders travelers.

See *mansions of the moon*.

Atar: Atar is one of the most important yazata angels in Zoroastrianism and is called the Angel of Fire. He is considered the son of Ahura Mazda, the supreme being in Zoroastrianism.

See *Ahura Mazda*, *yazata*, *Zoroastrianism*.

Atheniel (Alheniel): Atheniel is one of the twenty-eight angels who govern the mansions of the moon. Atheniel is responsible for Alchara, the twenty-seventh mansion. Atheniel performs both positive and negative tasks in this role. He increases harvests, ensures financial gain, and heals people who are sick. However, he also causes mischief, increases the length of prison sentences, and causes danger to sailors.

See *mansions of the moon*.

Authorities: The Authorities are an order of angels that correspond to the Powers or Virtues. They are not included in the hierarchy of angels developed by Dionysius the Areopagite. In the hierarchy compiled by St. John of Damascus, the Authorities are in sixth position, immediately after the Powers.

See *Dionysus the Areopagite, hierarchy of angels, Powers, Virtues*.

Avartiel: Avartiel helps protect pregnant women from miscarriages. In medieval times, pregnant women often wore protective amulets bearing the name of Avartiel as added protection. Both men and women wore amulets with Avartiel's name to ward off evil.

Avatar: The avatars are ten magical beings in Hinduism. They are similar to angels, as they act as intermediaries between God and mankind. However, they are not true angels but ten incarnations of the god Vishnu. They were manifested in both human and animal form. Their task is to fight evil and encourage goodness. The ten avatars are: Buddha, Kalki, Krishna, Kurma, Matsga, Narasimha, Parasurana, Rama, Vamana, and Varaha. Some people believe Krishna is a god rather than an avatar; these people then consider Krishna's brother, Balarama, to be the avatar.

Ave (Ar-vay): The Great Angel Ave is one of the most important of the Enochian Angels. He dictated the letters of the four Watchtower Tablets to Dr. John Dee and his scryer, Edward Kelley, and then explained what they meant.

See *Dee (Dr. John), Enochian angels*.

Azael: Azael, Azzah, and Uzzah were the three angels who, according to the Third Book of Enoch, were against God's decision to transform the prophet Enoch into the angel Metatron. However, they were smart enough to obey God's command to prostrate themselves before Metatron.

See *Azzah, Enoch, Metatron, Uzzah*.

Azariel: According to Jewish tradition, Azariel is the angel who governs all the waters of the earth. He is also one of the twenty-eight angels who govern the mansions of the moon. Azariel is responsible for Aldebaram, the fourth mansion. Azariel is a disruptive angel, causing problems with buildings, fountains, wells, and gold mines.

See *mansions of the moon*.

Azazel: "God Strengthens." Azazel was one of the leaders of the two hundred fallen angels who, according to Genesis 6:2–4, descended to earth and mated with mortal women. According to The First Book of Enoch, Azazel was one of the leaders of those fallen angels, called Grigori. While he was on earth, he taught women how to appear more attractive to men, using cosmetics and other devices. He also taught men how to make weapons so they'd be more effective at killing each other. Because of this, in 1 Enoch 2:8, God says, "On the day of the great judgement he shall be cast into the fire." In Jewish lore, Azazel is considered one of Satan's main supporters.

See *Enoch, fallen angels, Grigori, Satan*.

Azbuga (Azbuga YHWH, Azbugah, or Asbogha): Azbuga is one of the angel-princes in the Sarim and is one of the eight throne angels of judgment. His main task is to welcome the worthy into Heaven and clothe them with the Garment of Righteousness. He is said to be even more powerful than Metatron.

See *Metatron, Sarim*.

Azeruel: Azeruel is one of the twenty-eight angels who govern the mansions of the moon. Azeruel is responsible for Azubene, the sixteenth mansion. Although he encourages the ransoming of prisoners, Azeruel is generally negative as he hinders travel, weddings, harvests, and business.

See *mansions of the moon*.

Aziel: Aziel is one of the twenty-eight angels who govern the mansions of the moon. Aziel is in charge of Sadalabra, the twenty-fifth mansion. In this role, Aziel is a negative angel who encourages revenge and enmity, casts spells to prevent copulation, and prevents people from performing tasks they should be doing.

See *mansions of the moon.*

Azrael (Izrail): "Whom God Helps." Azrael lives in the Third Heaven and has the monumental task of recording everybody's names when they are born and erasing them again when they die. In angel magic, he is considered ruler of the planet Pluto, making him one of the planetary angels. In Jewish and Islamic lore, he is called *Izrail* and is the angel of death. This is probably because of his interest in reincarnation. Izrail does not know when someone will die. Allah writes the person's name on a leaf, which he drops from his throne. Izrail picks it up and collects the person's soul forty days later. Izrail has four thousand wings and four faces that are covered with a million veils. His body is made up of as many eyes and tongues as there are people living on earth. Every time Izrail blinks, it means someone has died. Izrail is so large that if all the water in the world were poured on his head, none would reach the ground. It would take a person 70,000 days to travel from one of his eyes to the other. Izrail is often depicted with one foot resting on a bridge that connects Heaven and Hell. People have to cross over this bridge to be judged.

Azrael became an angel of death in an interesting way. When God decided to create Adam, he sent Michael, Gabriel, and Israfil to earth to collect seven handfuls of dirt, which God was going to use to make the first man. The earth refused to accede to this request, as it believed mankind would cause only pain and suffering. Consequently, the three angels failed in their mission. God then sent Azrael down to earth. He forcibly extracted the dirt and returned to Heaven with it. To reward him for this, God decreed that Azrael would be responsible for releasing the human soul from the physical body at the moment of death.

Azrael can be called upon when exploring past lives, or when investigating psychic topics.

See *death (angel of)*, *Gabriel*, *Israfil*, *Michael*, *planetary angels*.

Azriel: Azriel is one of the destroying angels. He also helps God watch over the earth. Azriel may be another name for Azrael.

See *Azrael, destroying angels*.

Azzah (Azza): Azzah, Azael, and Uzzah were the three angels who objected when God decided to transform the prophet Enoch into the angel Metatron. However, they were quick to back down and welcomed Metatron to the ranks of angels, even though they teased him by calling him "a youth" because he was the youngest angel.

See *Azael, Metatron, Uzzah*.

Badpatiel: Badpatiel is one of the angels who protect pregnant women from miscarriage.

Baglis: Baglis helps people overcome addictions and other problems that have the potential to destroy people's lives. Baglis must be called upon during the second hour of the day.

Balthial (Balthiel): Balthial is the angel of forgiveness. Balthial can be invoked to help in situations when you should forgive someone else but find it difficult to do so. His task is to help people overcome feelings of rage, bitterness, jealousy, and envy. In the Third Book of Enoch, Balthiel is said to be the only angel who is able to help people overcome these destructive emotions.

    See *Enoch (Book of)*.

Baradiel: See *Barchiel*.

Baraqyal (Baraqel): In the First Book of Enoch, Baraqyal is listed as one of the ten leaders of the Grigori, the angels who came down to earth and cohabited with human women. Today, he is one of the fallen angels and lives in Hell. He is sometimes invoked by students of astrology who want to learn more about the art.

See *fallen angels, Grigori.*

Barattiel: According to the Third Book of Enoch, Barattiel is one of the most important angels in Heaven. He supports Arabot, the Seventh Heaven, on the tips of his fingers.

See *Arabot.*

Barbelo: Barbelo is a female archon and angel of prosperity and good fortune. You can call on Barbelo when you need more of these qualities in your life. You should also thank her for these blessings when you possess them.

See *archons.*

Barbiel: Barbiel is responsible for the month of October, and he looks after the interests of people born under the zodiac sign of Scorpio. Barbiel is a prince of both the choir of Archangels and the choir of Virtues. He is said to have an interest in astrology.

There appear to be two angels called Barbiel. The second one is a fallen angel who is one of the seven electors of Hell. This Barbiel is also one of the twenty-eight angels who govern the mansions of the moon. He is responsible for Archaam, the ninth mansion. He creates discord between people and causes problems with harvests and travelers.

See *Archangels, fallen angels, mansions of the moon, Virtues, zodiac (angels of the).*

Barchiel (Barakiel, Barachiel, Baraqiel, Barqiel, Baradiel, Barkiel, or Bardiel): "God's Blessings." Barchiel is ruler of the order of Seraphim, angel of February, prince of the Third Heaven, and a leading member of the Sarim. He looks after people born under the signs of Scorpio and Pisces. In the Third Book of Enoch he is called the angel of hail (as Baradiel) and the angel of lightning (as

Baraqiel). He is one of the eighteen Rulers of the Earth. Because of his importance in the angelic hierarchy, 496,000 ministering angels attend to Barchiel, according to the Book of Enoch. His role varies in different texts. He has been called one of the four Seraphim and one of the seven Archangels. He provides a positive outlook on life and good fortune. Gamblers desiring success with their wagers also invoke Barchiel, though they usually call him Barakiel.

See *Archangels*, *Enoch (Book of)*, *Rulers of the Earth*, *Sarim*, *Seraphim*, *zodiac (angels of the)*.

Bariel: Bariel is one of the princes of the Malakhim. He is, according to the Book of Raziel, one of the angels of Wednesday, Mercury's day. According to *The Lesser Key of Solomon*, he looks after the eleventh hour of every day and has a large staff of angels.

See *Malakhim*.

Barman (Bahman): In Persian cosmology, Barman was a great angel who looked after all the animals on earth, except for mankind. He was also the chief of the thirty angels who looked after each day of the month.

Bath Kol (Bat Qol): "Heavenly Voice." According to ancient tradition, it was Bath Kol who first asked Cain where his brother was. Although angels are genderless, Bath Kol is usually considered female. She is said to have visited Rabbi Simeon ben Yohai, reputed author of the Zohar, while he was in prison, or possibly during the twelve years he spent as a hermit living in a cave. Bath Kol helps people engaged in prophecy. Diviners can call out Bath Kol's name to help understand an omen or intuition; the next words the diviner hears are believed to contain the answer.

Beburos: According to the Book of Esdras, Beburos is one of the nine angels who will govern the world after the Day of Judgment. The others are: Aker, Arphugitonos, Gabriel, Gabuthelon, Michael, Raphael, Uriel, and Zebuleon.

See individual angels.

Beelzebub (Belzebub): Beelzebub was originally a Syrian god, but in the New Testament he is the "prince of devils" (Matthew 12:24; Mark 3:22). Beelzebub is sometimes referred to as the "lord of flies" and the "lord of chaos." Dante considered Beelzebub and Satan to be the same angel, but John Milton thought Beelzebub was "next to Satan in power and crime" (*Paradise Lost* 1:79).

See *Satan*.

Beliar (Beliel or Belial): Beliar is often called the Prince of Darkness. He was the first angel God created, and he was also the first fallen angel. St. Paul used his name as a synonym for the devil when he wrote: "And what concord hath Christ with Belial? or what part hath he that believeth with an infidel?" (2 Corinthians 6:15). In the apocryphal Gospel of St. Bartholomew, Beliar is said to live in Hell, where he is secured with fiery chains and held by 660 angels.

See *devil, fallen angels*.

Belphegor: At one time, Belphegor was a member of the order of Principalities. However, he became one of the fallen angels and is now a symbol of licentiousness in Hell. He is also interested in innovative inventions and new discoveries. Belphegor usually appears in the guise of an attractive young woman.

See *fallen angels, Principalities*.

Bene Elohim (Ben-ay El-o-him) **(Bene Elim or Bene ha-Elohim):** Originally, Bene Elohim meant "sons of God," and was the term used to describe angels in the Old Testament. Gradually, this term came to mean a choir of angels who sing the praises of God twenty-four hours a day. This choir is listed in the hierarchy of angels of Moses Maimonides and the Zohar. The Bene Elohim have been equated with both the Thrones and the Archangels. Some authorities consider them to be Grigori.

See *Archangels, Grigori, hierarchy of angels, Thrones*.

Bethelda: Bethelda is the angel who appeared to Geoffrey Hodson, the clairvoyant and Theosophist, in 1924. Bethelda told him that angels were divided into specialized groups, such as the angels of healing and the angels of nature.

See *Hodson (Geoffrey)*.

Bethnael: Bethnael is one of the twenty-eight angels who govern the mansions of the moon and is responsible for Abeda, the twenty-first mansion. Bethnael aids expansion and increase, and he helps travelers. He encourages divorce when relationships are failing.

See *mansions of the moon*.

Bethor: According to the *Arbatel of Magick*, a sixteenth-century grimoire, Bethor is one of the seven Olympian spirit angels who rule the 196 sections of Heaven. Bethor is responsible for 42 sections and has 29,000 legions of angels to help him do this. He is also responsible for the well-being of the planet Jupiter. Bethor ruled over the world from 60 BCE to AD 430.

See *Olympian spirits*.

Bodhisattvas: Bodhisattvas are angel-like beings in Mahayana Buddhism. They were originally people who have earned admittance to nirvana, but because of their love for humanity have decided to delay their arrival there to help other people reach salvation.

Boel (Boul or Bohel): According to some sources, Boel is one of the seven angels attending the Throne of God. However, according to the Zohar, Boel is one of the seven Thrones who look after the First Heaven. Boel also looks after the keys to the four corners of the earth. Consequently, if God commands it, he can unlock and open the gates to the Garden of Eden. Boel is also sometimes thought to be one of the rulers of the planet Saturn.

See *Throne of God, Thrones.*

Bonaventure, St.: Originally known as Giovanni di Fidanza, St. Bonaventure (1217–1274) was also known as "the Devout Teacher." He later became known as the Seraphic Doctor. St. Bonaventure was a contemporary and friend of St. Thomas Aquinas. Both had a strong interest in the hierarchy of angels. St. Bonaventure became minister general of the Franciscan Order in 1257. In 1273, he became cardinal bishop of Albano. St. Bonaventure wrote many works, including his *Life of St. Francis of Assisi* (1263). His most famous book is *The Soul's Journey into God* (1260). He received the inspiration for this book while meditating at the site on Mount La Verna, where St. Francis experienced a vision of a Seraph and received the stigmata. In *The Soul's Journey into God*, St. Bonaventure uses the hierarchy of angels as a template to show the soul's journey as it climbs to become as one with God. St. Bonaventure considered the lowest three levels of the hierarchy (Angels, Archangels, and Virtues) to correspond with human nature. The middle triad (Powers, Principalities, and Dominions) correspond with human effort, and the highest levels (Thrones, Cherubim, and Seraphim) correspond to the grace of God.

See *Angels, Aquinas (St. Thomas), Archangels, Cherubim, Dominions, hierarchy of angels, Powers, Principalities, Seraph, Seraphim, Thrones, Virtues.*

Botuliel: Botuliel is one of the ruling angels of the zodiac and is responsible for the sign of Virgo.

See *zodiac (angels of the).*

Buddhism, Angels of: Buddhists believe in reincarnation. Hopefully, over a number of lifetimes, a Buddhist can learn to let go of attachments and desires and ultimately achieve enlightenment. In Buddhism, there are angel-like beings called bodhisattvas, or "enlightened ones." Bodhisattvas are former humans who have delayed entering nirvana to help people who are currently alive attain enlightenment.

See *bodhisattvas*.

Burning Bush, Angel of the: It seems likely that the Angel of the Lord who spoke to Moses from a burning bush was actually God. In Exodus 3:6, the angel says: "I am the God of thy father, the God of Abraham, the God of Isaac, and the God of Jacob." However, both Archangel Michael and Zagzagel have been suggested as angel of the burning bush.

See *Archangels, Michael, Zagzagel*.

Cahatel (Kar-hay-tel) **(Cahathel):** Cahatel is one of the seventy-two Schemhamphoras, a group of angels who bear the various names of God found in Jewish scriptures. He is guardian angel of people born between April 26 and 30. Farmers call upon him to improve the quality and quantity of their crops.

See *guardian angels, Schemhamphoras.*

Caliel (Ka-lee-el) **(Calliel):** Caliel belongs to the choir of Thrones. He is one of the seventy-two Schemhamphoras, a group of angels who bear the various names of God found in Jewish scriptures. He is also guardian angel of people born between June 16 and 21. Caliel is an angel of joy and laughter, but he also helps people think before acting.

See *guardian angels, Schemhamphoras, Thrones.*

Camael: See *Chamuel.*

Cambiel (Cambriel or Kambriel): Cambiel is considered an Archangel and looks after the interests of people born under the zodiac sign of Aquarius. Cambiel is interested in science, technology, and anything new and progressive. He wears electric-blue robes and pours water onto the ground from a pottery pitcher. He has a blue jewel between his eyebrows.

See *Archangels, zodiac (angels of the)*.

Cassiel (Casiel, Caziel, Kassiel, or Cashiel): Cassiel, the angel of solitude and tears, is the lord of Saturn and the sign of Capricorn. This makes him one of the most important planetary angels. He is also ruler of the Seventh Heaven and a leading member of the choir of Powers. He helps people learn patience and encourages them to overcome long-standing obstacles and problems. He also provides serenity and teaches temperance. Cassiel is associated with karma, and he helps people understand the law of cause and effect. Because of his association with Saturn, Cassiel works slowly. Because it takes Saturn four years to orbit the Sun, Cassiel can take up to four years to resolve a problem. Fortunately, Raphael is willing to talk with Cassiel to speed up the process. Artists depict Cassiel as a fierce-looking man with a dark beard. He wears a crown and holds an arrow made from a feather. He sits astride a dragon.

See *Heavens, planetary angels, Powers, Raphael*.

Celestial Hierarchy: See *hierarchy of angels*.

Cerviel (Cervihel): Cerviel is one of the leaders of the choir of Principalities. According to Jewish legend, Cerviel is David's preceptor angel. God sent him to help David fight—and ultimately kill—Goliath.

See *preceptor angels, Principalities*.

Chadaqiel (Chedeqiel): Chadaqiel is the angel of the astrological sign of Libra. He helps Archangel Zuriel look after people of this sign.

See *Archangels, Zuriel*.

Chalkydri (Chal-kid-ree): In the Second Book of Enoch, the Chalkydri and the Phoenixes were said to be as important as the Seraphim and Cherubim. The Chalkydri have twelve wings, and they sing every morning as the sun rises. They live in the Fourth Heaven.

See *Cherubim, Phoenixes, Seraphim.*

Chamuel (Camael, Camiel, or Kemuel): "He Who Seeks God." Chamuel is head of the choir of Dominions and is one of the seven great Archangels. He has been given a number of other titles as well, including Ruler of Tuesday, Prince of the Seraphim, Chief of the Order of Powers, and Ruler of Mars. He is one of the leading members of the Sarim. Chamuel is one of God's favorite angels and is one of the Angels of the Presence. Chamuel is also one of the ten Kabbalistic Archangels. Some sources say Chamuel was the angel who comforted Jesus in the Garden of Gethsemane, although this is usually believed to have been Gabriel. Chamuel is also sometimes thought to be the dark angel who wrestled with Jacob for a full night (Genesis 32:24–30). Chamuel rights wrongs, soothes troubled minds, and provides justice. He can be called upon for any matters involving tolerance, understanding, forgiveness, and love. You should call on Chamuel whenever you need additional strength or are in conflict with someone else. Chamuel provides courage, persistence, and determination.

See *Archangels, dark angels, Dominions, Gabriel, Gethsemane (angel of), Powers, Presence (Angels of the), Sarim, Seraphim.*

Charmeine (Char-may-nay): Charmeine is an angel of joy, happiness, friendship, and love. You can call on Charmeine whenever you need these qualities.

Chassan (Chasen): Angel of Air. Chassan assists Archangel Raphael in his work. He lives in a tower in a special place in Heaven where it is always morning.

See *Archangels, Raphael.*

Chavakiah (Char-var-kee-yah): Chavakiah is one of the seventy-two Schemhamphoras, a group of angels who bear the various names of God found in Jewish scriptures. He is also the guardian angel of people born between September 13 and 17.

See *guardian angels, Schemhamphoras.*

Chayyiel (Chay-yee-el) **(Chayyliel H' or Hayyiel):** Chayyiel is an angel-prince and member of the Sarim. In the Jewish tradition, he is leader of the Hayyoth, who have the responsible task of carrying the throne of God. The Hayyoth are equated with the Cherubim in the Christian tradition. In the Third Book of Enoch, Chayyiel is described as being so large he could swallow the entire world in one mouthful.

See *Cherubim, Hayyoth.*

Cherub: Cherubs are the small, chubby, happy, child-like angels so beloved by Baroque artists. It's hard to believe that the word *cherub* was originally the singular form of the powerful Cherubim.

See *Cherubim.*

Cherubim: The Cherubim are the second-highest rank of angels in Dionysius' hierarchy of angels. Assyrian artists depicted them as winged beings with human or lion faces and the bodies of bulls, eagles, or sphinxes. Today, they are usually described as looking like large men with two, four, or six blue-colored wings. They are frequently depicted as wings and a head with no body. The prophet Ezekiel described the four Cherubim he saw in a vision:

> And every one had four faces, and every one had four wings. And their feet were straight feet; and the sole of their feet was like the sole of a calf's foot: and they sparkled like the colour of burnished brass. And they had the hands of a man under their wings on their four sides; and they four had their faces and their wings. Their wings were joined one to another; they turned not when they

went; they went every one straight forward. As for the likeness of their faces, they four had the face of a man, and the face of a lion, on the right side: and they four had the face of an ox on the left side; they four also had the face of an eagle. (Ezekiel 1:6–10)

According to Ezekial 10: 6–7, Cherubim live in fire and are frequently described as being fire-like. Their main task is to worship God and to act as his record keepers. They also act as guardians when required. After Adam and Eve were forced out of the garden of Eden, God "placed at the east of the garden of Eden Cherubims, and a flaming sword which turned every way, to keep the way of the tree of life" (Genesis 3:24). Satan may have been a prince of the Cherubim before his fall. Cherubim are God's record keepers and reflect his wisdom and divine intelligence. They pay careful attention to all the details. Two Cherubim were carved on the Ark of the Covenant. In Islamic legend, the Cherubim were created from the tears that Michael shed when he contemplated all the sins of humanity. Well-known members of the Cherubim include: Gabriel, Jophiel, Kerubiel, Ophaniel, Raphael, Uriel, and Zaphiel.

See *Ark of the Covenant, hierarchy of angels*, individual angels.

Chieftains: Chieftains is a term used to describe the seventy guardian angels that look after the different peoples of the earth.

See *guardian angels*.

Childbed Angels: Jewish tradition says there are seventy childbed angels who look after mothers during childbirth and protect the newly born babies from evil spirits.

Chista (Chisti): Chista is a female yazata. In Zoroastrianism, she teaches religious instruction.

See *yazata, Zoroastrianism*.

Choirs: In the hierarchy of angels, the various orders of angels are arranged in choirs, probably because one of the most important tasks an angel can perform is to sing the praises of God.

See *hierarchy of angels.*

Chosetiel (Cho-set-yee-el)**:** Chosetiel is one of the ruling angels of the zodiac and is responsible for the sign of Sagittarius.

See *zodiac (angels of the).*

Cochabiel (Coc-ha-bee-yee-el) **(Cochabiah):** In the Jewish Kabbalah, Cochabiel is the angel responsible for the planet Mercury. Cornelius Agrippa thought Cochabiel was one of the seven angels who attended the Throne of God.

See *Throne of God.*

Colopatiron (Col-op-a-tee-ron)**:** Colopatiron encourages people to act on their intuition. You can call on Colopatiron if you are trying to develop your psychic abilities.

Crocell (Cro-sel)**:** Crocell is a fallen angel and a former member of the choir of Powers. He now works for Satan as one of the rulers of Hell and has forty-eight legions of demons at his disposal. Apparently, Crocell told King Solomon that he intended to apologize to God and hoped to return to the choir of Powers.

See *fallen angels, Powers, Satan.*

Daena (De-na) **(Dena or Din):** Daena is a female yazata. She is the daughter of Ahura Mazda and Spenta Armaita. Daena looks after people's consciences, encouraging them to act honestly and ethically.
See *Ahura Mazda, Spenta Armaita, yazata, Zoroastrianism.*

Dagymiel: Dagymiel is one of the ruling angels of the zodiac and is responsible for the sign of Pisces.
See *zodiac (angels of the).*

Damabiah (Da-ma-bee-yah)**:** Damabiah is one of the seventy-two Schemhamphoras, a group of angels who bear the various names of God found in Jewish scriptures. Damabiah is also guardian angel of people born between February 10 and 14. Damabiah offers the benefit of his wisdom to people who sincerely ask for it.
See *guardian angels, Schemhamphoras.*

Damascus, St. John of: St. John of Damascus (c.675–c.749) was a theologian and writer in the Eastern Church. He was born in Damascus and spent the latter part of his life studying, writing, and worshiping in a monastery near Jerusalem.

Daniel (Dar-nee-el): "God is my judge." Daniel belongs to the order of Principalities and, according to the Book of Raziel, is one of the guardian angels of Sunday. Daniel is one of the seventy-two Schemhamphoras, a group of angels who bear the various names of God found in Jewish scriptures. He is also guardian angel of people born between November 28 and December 2. Daniel helps people to see the inner beauty in others.

See *guardian angels*, *Principalities*, *Schemhamphoras*.

Dark Angels: Satan and his followers are sometimes referred to as dark angels. The term is also used to describe the angel who fought all night long with Jacob at Peniel:

> And Jacob was left alone; and there wrestled a man with him until the breaking of the day. And when he saw that he prevailed not against him, he touched the hollow of his thigh; and the hollow of Jacob's thigh was out of joint, as he wrestled with him. And he said, Let me go, for the day breaketh. And he said, I will not let thee go, except thou bless me. And he said unto him, What is thy name? And he said, Jacob. And he said, Thy name shall be called no more Jacob, but Israel: for as a prince hast thou more power with God and with men, and hast prevailed. And Jacob asked him, and said, Tell me, I pray thee, thy name. And he said, Wherefore is it that thou dost ask after my name? And he blessed him there. And Jacob called the name of the place Peniel: for I have seen God face to face, and my life is preserved. (Genesis 32:24–30)

No one knows who this angel was, although several angels have been suggested. These include: Michael, Chamuel, Metatron, Peniel, Sammael, and Uriel.

See *Satan*, individual angels.

Day, Angels of the: Angels and Archangels have been assigned to the different days of the week. Magicians used this information to help them perform their rituals at the most propitious times.

Sunday: Raphael (Archangel) and Michael (angel)
Monday: Gabriel (Archangel and angel of the day)
Tuesday: Chamuel (Archangel) and Samael (angel)
Wednesday: Michael (Archangel) and Raphael (angel)
Thursday: Tzaphiel (Archangel) and Sachiel (angel)
Friday: Haniel (Archangel) and Anael (angel)
Saturday: Tzaphiel (Archangel) and Cassiel (angel)

See *Archangels, planetary angels,* individual angels, *week (angels of the)*.

Death, Angel of: The concept of an angel of death is widespread, and there are several references to destroying angels in the Bible (Exodus 12:23, 2 Samuel 24:16, Proverbs 16:14, Isaiah 37:36, and Jeremiah 9:20). The angel of death has been associated with Satan, and this connection is reflected in the folktales of many countries. In many Jewish stories, the angel of death arrives on a couple's wedding night, and the story involves the proposed victim somehow fooling or cheating the angel of death. There are fifteen named angels of death in Jewish lore. They are: Abaddon, Adriel, Af, Azrael, Gabriel, Hemah, Kafziel, Kesef, Leviathan, Malak Ha-Mavet, Mashit, Metatron, Sammael, Yehudiah, and Yetzer Hara.

Azrael is the Islamic angel of death. He has a number of helpers, including Malak al mawt, the keeper of Hell, who is a Malaika angel. For Christians, Michael fulfils the role of angel of death.

There are also gods of death. The ancient Etruscans had a god of death called Charon. He had enormous wings and a beaked nose, making him look like a gigantic bird. In addition to carrying souls to Hades, he also looked after the underworld. The ancient Greeks had a god of death called Thanatos. He visited humans at the moment of death and carried them to Hades.

See *destroying angels,* individual angels, *Malaika.*

Dee, Dr. John: Dr. John Dee (1527–1608) was an English astrologer, magician, mathematician, philosopher, and alchemist who communicated with angels on many occasions. He was an influential man in Elizabethan England, even advising Queen Elizabeth I on the most suitable date for her coronation. It is highly likely that he performed espionage work for Queen Elizabeth, too. He was involved in many activities, including calendar reform, cartography, geography, and navigation. Dee owned the largest library in England, and people came from all over Europe to visit his library and to talk with him. Dee is best remembered today for his interest in angels. He, and Edward Kelley, a gifted scryer, contacted the angelic realms and Dee recorded hundreds of pages of experiences in his journals. Dee saw and conversed with Uriel on at least two occasions. Arguably, Dee's greatest achievement was receiving the Enochian language, or the language of angels, from the Enochian angels.

See *Enochian angels*, *Enochian language*, *Uriel*.

Deliel: Deliel is one of the ruling angels of the zodiac and is responsible for the sign of Aquarius.

See *zodiac (angels of the)*.

Demon: The word *demon* comes from the Greek *daimon*, a type of angel or spirit who interceded between the gods and humans. There were good and bad daimons who tried to influence people's behavior. Socrates, the Greek philosopher, had a daimon that inspired him to speak the truth and to search for the truth in everything he did.

The word *demon* is commonly used to describe a fallen angel. A demon's task is to help Satan in his war against God and everything that is good. In Islam, demons are called *shaitans*, or "black angels."

Demons helped King Solomon finish his temple. God ordered Archangel Raphael to take a special pentagram ring to King Solomon. This ring enabled the king to overpower the demons and force them to work on his temple. Raphael also outwitted the demon Asmodeus in the Book of Tobit.

See *Archangels, Asmodeus, fallen angels, Raphael, Satan.*

Destroying Angels (Angels of Destruction or Angels of Punishment): Destroying angels act on God's behalf to punish people who deserve it. Archangel Uriel is in charge of the destroying angels, and he has many assistants, including Azriel, Chamuel, Dumah, Harbonah, Hemah, and Kesef. Chamuel was in charge of twelve thousand destroying angels. An account of the destroying angels who were sent to Jerusalem is related in Ezekiel 9:1–11. Two destroying angels brought down Sodom and Gomorrah, and one angel of destruction killed 185,000 soldiers in the Assyrian army (2 Kings 19:35). Mediator angels are almost diametrically opposite to destroying angels.

See *Archangels, mediator angels,* individual angels.

Devil: The devil is God's main enemy. He has a variety of names, the best known of which is Satan. According to Judaic and Christian lore, it was the devil who caused Adam and Eve to be thrown out of the Garden of Eden.

See *Satan.*

Dina: According to the Kabbalah, Dina is one of the guardians of the Torah, and she has a special interest in learning and wisdom.

Dionysius the Areopagite: In the Acts of the Apostles 17:34, Dionysius the Areopagite was converted by St. Paul. This Dionysius was a judge of the court of the Areopagus. He ultimately became bishop of Athens. However, the books attributed to Dionysius were written in the late fifth or early sixth centuries by an unknown author who presumably used this pseudonym in the hope that his writings would be taken more seriously. It took almost a thousand years before people realized that Dionysius the author could not be the same Dionysius who was converted by St. Paul. Dionysius the author was probably a Syrian monk. Scholars have come up with several possibilities for the author's true name. Peter Fuller, who was Patriarch of Antioch from 471 until 488 is arguably the most likely possibility. Dionysius' writings include *The Celestial Hierarchy*, *The Divine Names*, and *The Mystical Theology*. He was the first person to use the word "hierarchy" and devised the most influential hierarchy of angels.

See *hierarchy of angels.*

Dirachiel (Di-rash-yee-el): Dirachiel is said to be associated with the seven electors of Hell. If so, he is a fallen angel. Dirachiel is also one of the twenty-eight angels who govern the mansions of the moon. He is responsible for Athanna, the sixth mansion. Dirachiel helps hunters, princes seeking revenge, and people who are besieging cities. However, he also destroys harvests and hinders physicians in their work.

See *fallen angels, mansions of the moon.*

Djibril (Jib-ril) **(Jibril or Jibra'il):** Djibril is the Islamic name for Archangel Gabriel. In the Koran, he is called "the faithful spirit." Although Djibril is a huge angel, he usually appears as a muscular, heavy-set man, wearing green clothes and a silk turban. He has six hundred or more beautiful green wings that cover most of the horizon. His face is illuminated, and the phrase "There is no God but God, and Muhammad is the Prophet of God" is written between his eyes. Djibril first appeared to Muhammad when he was meditating on a mountain close to Mecca. Djibril dictated the Koran to Muhammad during the Night of Glory. He also took Muhammad on a guided tour of the various Heavens. Djibril is sometimes called Bringer of Good News and Faithful Servant.

See *Archangels, Gabriel.*

Dominions (Dominations): St. Paul mentioned the choirs of angels, including the Dominions, in his Epistle of Paul the Apostle to the Colossians 1:16: "For by him were all things created, that are in

Heaven, and that are in earth, visible and invisible, whether they be thrones, or dominions, or principalities, or powers: all things were created by him, and for him." The Dominions are the fourth most important rank of angels in Dionysius the Areopagite's hierarchy of angels. They work in Heaven as middle-level executives, deciding what needs to be done and issuing the necessary orders to ensure that the universe works the way it should. Artists usually depict the Dominions in green and gold robes. They have two wings. They carry a seal containing a monogram of Jesus in their right hands and a staff with a cross on the top in their left hands. The chiefs of the Dominions are said to include Hashmal, Zadkiel, Muriel, and Zacharael.

See *Dionysius the Areopagite, hierarchy of angels*, individual angels.

Donquel: Donquel is one of the angels of Venus. Donquel is an angel of love and romance. He works for both men and women but is more usually called upon by men seeking the love of a good woman. Donquel wears a light-blue robe with a green-and-yellow sash over one shoulder. He wears a copper necklace with a heart-shaped pendant on it.

Dragon: Satan is called "the great dragon" in the Bible: "And the great dragon was cast out, that old serpent, called the devil, and Satan, which deceiveth the whole world: he was cast out into the earth, and his angels were cast out with him" (Revelation 12:9). Archangel Michael is often depicted with one foot resting on a dragon he has slain, showing the power of good over evil.

See *Archangels, Michael, Satan*.

Dubbiel (Dobiel or Dubiel): Dubbiel was originally the guardian angel of Persia. When God became angry with Gabriel, Dubbiel temporarily took over Gabriel's role and allowed the Persians to expand their empire by conquering other countries. After twenty-one days of disgrace, Gabriel resumed his original position and

Dubbiel was demoted. Eventually, Dubbiel, along with all the other guardian angels of different countries (except for Michael, guardian angel of Israel), became fallen angels. From his home in Hell, Dubbiel records all of the sins of Israel, hoping that God will expunge the country and all its inhabitants from the world.

See *fallen angels, Gabriel, guardian angels, Michael.*

Dumah (Douma): Dumah was originally the guardian angel of Egypt. Along with the other guardian angels of seventy countries (with the exception of Michael, guardian angel of Israel), Dumah became a fallen angel. Since then, he has been the angel of the stillness of death, the angel of silence, and the angel of punishment. He is one of the leaders of the destroying angels, and according to the Zohar, he is Prince of Hell and has ten thousand angels of destruction beneath him.

See *destroying angels, fallen angels, guardian angels, Michael.*

Dynamis (Dunamis): In the Gnostic tradition, Dynamis is both an aeon and one of the rulers of the archons. He is the personification of divine power.

See *aeons, archons.*

Earth, Angel of: See *Phorlach*.

Eblis: Eblis is the Arabic and Persian equivalent of Satan. Before his
fall, he was the Heavenly treasurer. Today, he rules the Peri.
See *Peri, Satan*.

Ecanus: Ecanus helps people who are involved in writing. He can be
invoked by people intending to make a career in literary pursuits.
In the Book of Esdras, Ecanus was one of five angels who, on the
orders of God, transcribed the books dictated to them by Esdras.

Egibiel: Egibiel is one of the twenty-eight angels who govern the
mansions of the moon. Egibiel is responsible for Alchas, the eighteenth mansion. In this role, he is a destructive angel causing
discord and disharmony, especially between people in power. He
helps people who seek revenge. However, he also frees prisoners
and helps in the maintenance of large buildings.
See *mansions of the moon*.

Eiael (Ay-ya-el) **(Ejael or Eyael):** Eiael is one of the seventy-two Schemhamphoras, a group of angels who bear the various names of God found in Jewish scriptures. He is the angel of both happiness and occult knowledge. Eiael also aids longevity and a positive outlook on life. He is the guardian angel of people born between February 20 and 24.

See *guardian angels, Schemhamphoras.*

Elders: According to St. John, twenty-four angels sit upon thrones that circle the Throne of God. These angels are known as the Elders. Many scholars believe the Elders are a special, possibly secret, order of angels who are close to God and help him with delicate tasks. According to the Second Book of Enoch, the Elders live in the First Heaven. St. John also saw the Elders in a vision: "And immediately I was in the spirit: and behold, a throne was set in Heaven, and *one* sat on the throne. And he that sat was to look upon like a jasper and a sardine stone: and *there was* a rainbow round about the throne, in sight like unto an emerald. And round about the throne *were* four and twenty seats: and upon the seats I saw four and twenty elders sitting, clothed in white raiment; and they had on their heads crowns of gold" (Revelation 4:2–4).

See *Throne of God.*

Elemiah (El-em-ee-yah) **(Elemijel):** According to the Kabbalah, Elemiah is one of the eight Seraphim of the Tree of Life. Elemiah belongs to the Schemhamphoras, a group of seventy-two angels who bear the various names of God found in Jewish scriptures. Elemiah is the guardian angel of people born between April 5 and 9. Elemiah looks after travellers, particularly people travelling over sea. Elemiah can also be invoked by anyone involved in inner growth and spiritual pursuits.

See *guardian angels, Schemhamphoras*

Elijah: See *Sandalphon.*

Elim: "Mighty Ones." The Elim are a superior class of angels mentioned in the Third Book of Enoch. They are in seventh position in the hierarchy of angels mentioned in the Zohar.

See *hierarchy of angels*.

Elimiel: According to the Kabbalah, Elimiel is the angel who looks after the moon.

El-Karubiyan: El-Karubiyan are the Cherubim in the Islamic tradition. They unceasingly praise and worship God.

See *Cherubim*.

Elohim: The word *elohim* means "Jehovah" (YHWH) in Hebrew. The Elohim are one of the ten choirs of angels mentioned in the Key of Solomon and are listed in the hierarchy of angels of Moses Maimonides, Pico della Mirandola, and the Zohar. They are referred to as "shining beings." The word *elohim* also refers to the Angels of the Presence. In addition, the Elohim are the seven great angels in Gnosticism. To complicate matters still further, *elohim* is also the Hebrew name for God.

See *hierarchy of angels*, *Presence (Angels of the)*.

Elomnia (Elomina): Your fortunes may be about to improve if you happen to see an angel called Elomnia. Elomnia appears as a child or a small woman, wearing green and silver clothes and a wreath of bay leaves bedecked with green and white flowers. After she has gone, Elomnia leaves a pleasant, sweet odor behind. Elomnia can be invoked to help control losses and to gain money.

Emmanuel: Saint Umiltà of Faenzà (1226–1310) had two guardian angels: Emmanuel and Sapiel. They became her closest friends and confidantes. *Emmanuel* means "God is with us." Emmanuel may be a Seraph, as Saint Umiltà described him as fiery, dazzling, and incandescent. He also lived in the Seventh Heaven, within sight of God.

See *Sapiel*, *Seraph*.

Enediel: Enediel is one of the twenty-eight angels who govern the mansions of the moon. Enediel is responsible for Allothaim, the second mansion. Enediel helps people find treasure and aids travelers. He is involved with agriculture, particularly planting and sowing. In medicine, he impedes purgatives. He also ensures that prisoners are securely held.

See *mansions of the moon.*

Enoch: See *Metatron.*

Enoch, Book of: The Book of Enoch is one of the main sources of information on angels, particularly the fallen angels. It was written by a number of authors in the last two centuries BCE. Tertullian (c.160–220), an important theologian and author, thought the Book of Enoch was divinely inspired and had been preserved by Noah at the time of the Great Flood. Origen (c.185–c.254), the biblical scholar, thought it was just as important as the Psalms. However, the Book of Enoch was always controversial, partly because Enoch placed the fallen angels in different parts of Heaven. The traditional Christian view was that Heaven was above, and Hell below. Consequently, it was impossible for the fallen angels to be living in different parts of Heaven. Partly because of this, St. Jerome (c.342–420), one of the fathers of the early church and the first to translate the Bible from Hebrew into Latin, declared them apocryphal. After this, the books of Enoch were almost forgotten until James Bruce, a Scottish explorer, found three copies of it in Abyssinia in 1773. He kept one for himself and donated the other two to the Bodleian Library in Oxford and the Librairie Bibliothèque in Paris.

See *Apocrypha, fallen angels.*

Enochian Angels: The Enochian angels are the angels that Dr. John Dee and his scryer, Edward Kelley, communicated with between 1581 and 1587. Most of the information was communicated in the Enochian language. The Great Angel Ave dictated most of the information that came through. However, there were others, including Madimi, who appeared as a young girl with golden hair. Dee became so fond of Madimi that he named one of his daughters after her. Madimi's mother, who never gave her name, was the most important angel to communicate with Dee and Kelley. She called herself "I AM." I AM did not communicate with the scryers directly but sent information through her children. The four great Archangels—Michael, Gabriel, Raphael, and Uriel—also provided information to the two men. An angel called Nalvage passed on important information about angelic hierarchies.

In the Enochian system, there are angels of the four directions, which are symbolized as watchtowers. These watchtowers are large grid-like tables containing letters that can be arranged to form the names of different angels. Each watchtower is governed by six Elders, which relate to the twenty-four Elders mentioned in The Revelation of St. John the Divine. Below them is an entire hierarchy of Archangels and angels.

Dee and Kelley recorded a huge amount of information from the angels but did not make practical use of it. Some three hundred years later, S. L. MacGregor Mathers incorporated Enochian magic, including the angels, into the teachings of the Hermetic Order of the Golden Dawn. As a result of this, more people are interested in the Enochian angels today than ever before.

See *Angels, Archangels, Dee (Dr. John), Elders, Enochian language, Gabriel, I AM, Madimi, Michael, Nalvage, Raphael, Uriel.*

Enochian Language: On March 26, 1582, the Enochian angels who live in the watchtowers and Aethyrs in the far reaches of the universe started communicating the Enochian language, or the language of the angels, to Dr. John Dee and his scryer, Edward Kelley. The Enochian angels were, apparently, the same angels who had taught the prophet Enoch, who later became the angel Metatron. The angels told Dee that the Enochian language was spoken in Heaven before Adam and Eve were forced out of Paradise. Enoch was taught this language when he became an angel, which is why it is called Enochian. The alphabet contains twenty-one hieroglyphic letters, which are written from right to left. The Enochian language has its own characters and syntax and is unrelated to any other language.

See *Dee (Dr. John)*, *Enochian angels*, *Metatron*.

Eraziel (Araziel): Eraziel is the angel of Taurus and helps Archangel Asmodel look after people born under this sign.

See *Archangels*, *Asmodel*.

Erelim (Arelim): In Jewish mysticism, the Erelim are huge angels who look after plants and vegetation. They observe what is happening in the natural world and report their findings directly to God. This is easy for them to do, as they apparently have seventy thousand heads, each head having seventy thousand mouths. Each mouth has seventy thousand tongues, and each tongue then has seventy thousand sayings. The Erelim are made of white fire. Raziel is generally considered chief of the choir of Erelim.

Erellim (Erelim, Aralim, or Arelim): "The Valiant ones." The Erellim are a choir of angels mentioned in the Third Book of Enoch and other Jewish texts. The word *erellim* is often considered to be another name for the choir of Thrones. Maimonides (1138–1204), the great Spanish philosopher, listed the Erellim in his ten orders of angels. The term comes from the Bible: "Behold, their valiant ones [erellim] shall cry without: the ambassadors of peace shall weep bitterly" (Isaiah 33:7).

See *Thrones*.

Erethe: Erethe is a female yazata angel in Zoroastrianism. She personifies honesty and truth.

See *yazata*, *Zoroastrianism*.

Ergediel: Ergediel is one of the twenty-eight angels who govern the mansions of the moon. Ergediel is in charge of Alchureth, the fourteenth mansion. Ergediel cures the sick and strengthens the bonds of love between married couples. He helps people who are traveling by sea, but hinders those who are traveling over land.

See *mansions of the moon.*

Eth: "Time." Eth is the angel who looks after time and ensures that everything happens when it should. Eth can be invoked for guidance and help when one's patience is exhausted.

Ethnarchs: God was so upset at the building of the Tower of Babel that he sent humans to many different countries and gave them different languages to speak. He also promoted seventy angels and made them guardian angels of the new countries. They were called ethnarchs. Unfortunately, with only one exception—Michael, the guardian angel of Israel—they took their support for their various countries too far and became fallen angels.

See *guardian angels, fallen angels, Michael.*

Exordo: Exordo is the term devised by Alan of Lille for his hierarchy of antiangels. These are the fallen angels who constantly wage war on the good angels and all of humanity. Alan of Lille listed and described the attributes of his exordo:

1. Antiseraphim (who try to deny humanity the love of God and people)
2. Anticherubim (who try to deny humanity the knowledge of God)
3. Antithrones (who try to tempt humanity away from sound judgment)
4. Antidominions (who try to tempt humanity into irrational governance)
5. Antiprincipalities (who encourage tyranny)
6. Antipowers (who try to tempt humanity into evil)

7. Antivirtues (who use illusion and trickery to make fun of humanity)
8. Antiarchangels (who encourage false prophecy and doctrines)
9. Antiangels (who discourage care of others and spread false rumors about God)

See *Alan of Lille, fallen angels, hierarchy of angels.*

Ezekiel: Ezekiel is an angel of transformation. He helps people turn their lives around and create a positive outlook on life.

Ezgadi: Ezgadi is one of the angels who can be invoked for protection while traveling.

Fallen Angels: The fallen angels are angels who have fallen from grace and are now imprisoned in Hell or one of the two punishment areas of Heaven. There are two main groups of fallen angels. The Grigori, or watchers, were angels who became so fascinated with human women that they came to earth and copulated with them. Satan and his supporters comprise the other main group.

When God ordered the angels to bow down to Adam, nearly a third of the angels in Heaven refused. This led to the war in Heaven. Archangel Michael led the Heavenly hosts into battle against Satan and his supporters. After being soundly defeated, Satan and the rebels were expelled from Heaven. The biblical record reads: "And there was war in Heaven: Michael and his angels fought against the dragon; and the dragon fought and his angels, and prevailed not; neither was their place found any more in Heaven. And the great dragon was cast out, that old serpent, called the devil, and Satan, which deceiveth the whole world: he was cast out into the earth, and his angels were cast out with him" (Revelation 12:7–9). It is interesting to note that fallen angels are not mentioned in the Old Testament. Although Satan is usually named as the leader of the fallen angels, some of the apocryphal texts suggest other angels in this role, including Azazel, Beliar, Beelzebub, and Sammael. In Islam, Iblis is leader of the fallen angels.

See *Archangels*, individual angels, *Grigori*, *Satan*, *war in Heaven*, *watchers*.

Feast Days: Until 1969, the Roman Catholic Church had special days to celebrate the great Archangels Michael, Gabriel, and Raphael. The feast day for Michael was September 29; Gabriel's was March 24; and Raphael's October 24. Since 1969, all three Archangels are venerated on September 29. Because he is not mentioned by name in the canonical scriptures, Uriel did not have a feast day in the Catholic Church. However, he does not miss out entirely. The Orthodox churches in Egypt and Ethiopia venerate Uriel on July 28. The Catholic Church has a feast day for guardian angels on October 2.

See *Archangels*, *Gabriel*, *guardian angels*, *Michael*, *Raphael*.

Fire, Angel of: See *Aral*.

Focalor (Fork-al-yor) **(Forcalor):** Focalor is a fallen angel who lives in Hell, where he is in charge of thirty legions of demons. He was originally a member of the order of Thrones.

See *demon*, *fallen angels*, *Thrones*.

Forcas (Furcas): Forcas is a fallen angel. He is considered a duke in Hell, where he is in charge of twenty-nine legions of demons. He spends most of his time teaching logic and mathematics. He is sometimes invoked by people wanting to become invisible or to locate lost property.

See *fallen angels*.

Forces: St. John of Damascus created a hierarchy of angels that placed a choir of angels he called Forces in fourth position. Their role is to look after earthly concerns.

See *Damascus (St. John of)*, *hierarchy of angels*.

Fravashis (Favashis): In Zoroastrianism, fravashis are guardian angels that accompany people through life. They can guide and advise but cannot act directly. Zoroastrians believe God created fravashis before creating the universe. Originally, fravashis guarded and looked after Heaven, but after mankind was invented, they volunteered to come to earth to look after people. After someone dies, his or her relatives need to remember the person's fravashi, as he will continue to look after and bless the descendants of his charge. Fravashis are usually depicted as beings of human form riding on winged circles that have streamers hanging beneath them.

See *guardian angels*, *Zoroastrianism*, *Zoroastrian angels*.

Gabamiah: See *Jabamiah*.

Gabriel (Gab-ree-el): "God Is My Strength." Gabriel, one of the four named Archangels in the Hebraic tradition, is the Angel of the Annunciation, a leading member of the Sarim, and God's main messenger. Gabriel is one of the three angels who are mentioned by name in the Bible. (The others are Michael and Raphael. Raphael figures in the Book of Tobit, one of the fifteen books that make up the Apocrypha, which is part of the Roman Catholic Bible.) Gabriel is the ruler of the Cherubim, and he sits on God's left-hand side. He is also said to be one of the princes of the choir of Virtues. He is often known as the Angel of the Annunciation, Angel of Mercy, Angel of Revelation, Chief Ambassador to Humanity, Divine Herald, Prince of Justice, and Trumpeter of the Last Judgment. Gabriel is the angel of purification, guidance, and prophecy. He is also one of the twenty-eight angels who rule over the mansions of the moon. He is responsible for Alchatay, the fifth mansion.

In this role, he provides good health, education for students, and ensures that travellers return home safely from their journeys.

Gabriel's first appearance in the Bible is when he visited Daniel to explain a vision (Daniel 8:16). In the New Testament, he visits Zacharias to announce the birth of John the Baptist (Luke 1:11–22). Gabriel's most famous message occurred when he told the Virgin Mary she would give birth to Jesus Christ (Luke 1:26–33).

Jewish legend includes a fascinating story about Gabriel and an angel called Dubbiel, who was then guardian angel of Persia. God became annoyed with Israel and ordered Gabriel to kill all the Jews by pouring burning coals onto them. Any survivors were to be killed by the Babylonians. Gabriel felt sorry for the Israelites and asked the laziest angel in Heaven to pass the burning coals to him. This angel was so slow that the coals were almost cold when Gabriel threw them at Israel. Gabriel then convinced the Babylonians that it was better to force the Jews into Babylon than it was to kill them. God was furious at this action and demoted Gabriel from his position as chief minister in Heaven, replacing him with Dubbiel. Dubbiel wasted no time in helping the Persian people at the expense of every other country. Twenty-one days later, when God was having a meeting with his leading angels, Gabriel popped his head into the room and made an astute comment. God was thrilled with this and immediately restored Gabriel to his former position.

Another charming legend about Gabriel says that he teaches unborn children about Heaven while they are in the womb. Just before they are born, he touches them above the upper lip so they cannot remember what he told them until they die. Gabriel's touch creates the philtrum, or cleft, between the upper lip and nose.

In Jewish lore, Gabriel caused milk to flow from the infant Abraham's right little finger. This enabled him to feed himself while abandoned in a cave.

In Islam, Gabriel is called Djibril. Muslims believe Gabriel dictated the Koran to Muhammad.

See *Annunciation (angel of the)*, *Apocrypha*, *Archangels*, *Cherubim*, *Djibril*, *Dubbiel*, *guardian angels*, *mansions of the moon*, *Michael*, *Raphael*, *Sarim*, *Virtues*.

Gabriella: Gabriella is the female version of Gabriel. According to Jewish tradition, Gabriella is the only female Archangel. One indication that Gabriella is female is that she sits on the left-hand side of God. She also looks after the souls of unborn babies and teaches them for the nine months before they are born. Immediately before they are born, Gabriella touches them on the upper lip to make them forget what he taught them about Heaven until they die. The cleft beneath the nose is caused by Gabriella's touch. Gabriella's involvement with conception and babies has led many people to hypothesize that Gabriel is actually Gabriella. However, all of this debate ignores the fact that angels are spiritual beings who are believed to be genderless.

See *Gabriel*.

Gabuthelon: According to the Book of Esdras, Gabuthelon is one of the nine angels who will govern the world after the Day of Judgment. The others are: Aker, Arphugitonos, Beburos, Gabriel, Michael, Raphael, Uriel, and Zebuleon.

See *individual angels*.

Gadreel: Gadreel is one of the leaders of the Grigori. Some sources claim he seduced Eve, and he is believed to have taught mankind how to make and use weapons to fight each other.

See *Grigori*.

Galgalliel (Galgaliel): In the Third Book of Enoch, Galgalliel is said to be one of the two ruling angels of the sun. Ninety-six angels help him ensure that the sun follows its daily path. Galgalliel is a member of the Sarim and ruler of the Galgallim.

See *Galgallim*, *Rulers of the Earth*, *Sarim*.

Galgallim (Galgallin): Galgallim is an alternative name for the choir of Thrones. It is derived from the Hebrew word for "wheels," which is *galgal*. The Thrones are seen as wheels that circle the throne of God (Ezekiel 10:12–13). The leader of the Galgallim is Rikbiel.

See *Rikbiel, Thrones.*

Gatekeeper Angels: The first known gatekeeper angels were the Cherubim who were posted at the entrance of the Garden of Eden to prevent Adam and Eve from getting back in. Hadraniel, the angel who is more than two million miles tall, stands as the powerful gatekeeper angel at the entrance to Heaven. In Islam, Ridwan serves as the gatekeeper to Paradise.

See *Cherubim, Hadraniel, Ridwan.*

Gavreel: Gavreel is one of the guardians of the Second Heaven. (Some authorities believe he looks after the Fourth Heaven.) Gavreel helps provide inner peace when required. He also helps create harmony in potentially difficult and stressful situations.

Gazardiel: According to Jewish legend, Gazardiel is one of the angels responsible for sunrise and sunset. Because he is involved with the start of every day, he can be invoked for any new beginnings.

See *Gazriel.*

Gazriel: Gazriel can be called upon to ensure the success of any enterprise. Gazriel and Gazardiel may well be the same angel.

See *Gazardiel.*

Gedobonai: In *The Lesser Key of Solomon*, Gedobonai is said to be an angel who can help people control any potential financial losses or gains. He usually appears as a small woman, or a child, wearing green and silver clothes, with a wreath of bay leaves around his neck.

Geliel: Geliel is one of the twenty-eight angels who govern the mansions of the moon. He is in charge of Sadahacha, the twenty-second mansion. Geliel helps cure illnesses and assists prisoners to escape.

See *mansions of the moon.*

Geniel: Geniel is one of the twenty-eight angels who govern the mansions of the moon. He is in charge of Alnath, the first mansion. He helps ensure the success of travels and is involved with the dispensing of medicines, especially laxatives. Geniel sometimes also creates discord.

See *mansions of the moon.*

Gethsemane, Angel of: The angel of Gethsemane is the unnamed angel who gave comfort to Jesus in the hours before his arrest. The Gospel of St. Luke reads: "And there appeared an angel unto him from Heaven, strengthening him. And being in an agony he prayed more earnestly: and his sweat was as it were great drops of blood falling down to the ground" (St. Luke 22:43–44). Although this angel is not named, tradition says it was Archangel Gabriel. A less-likely possibility is the Archangel Chamuel.

See *Archangels, Chamuel, Gabriel.*

Geush Urvan (Gay-oosh Er-vahn): Geush Urvan is a yazata who assists Vohu Manah in looking after the well-being of all animals.

See *Vohu Manah, yazata, Zoroastrianism.*

Gloria In Excelsis Deo: This Latin phrase means "Glory to God in the highest," and was part of the song angels sang to the shepherds in the fields after announcing the birth of Christ. The biblical account reads: "And suddenly there was with the angel a multitude of the Heavenly host praising God, and saying, Glory to God in the highest, and on earth peace, good will toward men" (Luke 2:13–14).

God's Servants: This is another name for angels, and the term was taken from St. Paul's Epistle to the Hebrews: "Are they not all ministering spirits, sent forth to minister for them who shall be heirs of salvation?" (Hebrews 1:14). The word *minister* in this verse means "serve." Consequently, angels are God's servants.

See *Angel*.

Godiel: Godiel is one of the ruling angels of the zodiac and is responsible for the sign of Capricorn.

See *zodiac (angels of the)*.

Graphiel: Graphiel is the angel of Mars and helps Archangel Zamael look after the red planet.

See *Archangels, Zamael*.

Grigori (Watchers): The Grigori are fallen angels. At one time, the Grigori were some of the most loving and responsible of all angels. According to the Book of Jubilees, God sent them to earth to teach mankind how to farm and manage the vast selection of bounties from nature. Some of the Grigori fell in love with human women, and their offspring were known as Nephilim, huge giants who had evil natures. They were largely exterminated during the Great Flood. The fallen Grigori are imprisoned in Heaven. Jewish tradition says Shemhazai was the leader of the Grigori. The most important Grigori, according to the Book of Enoch, are: Asbeel, Gadreel, Jeqon, Kasbeel, Kasdeja, and Penemue (1 Enoch, 69:4–15).

See *fallen angels*, individual angels, *Nephilim, Shemhazai*.

Guardian angels: The concept of guardian angels who look after individuals, churches, cities, and even nations, is extremely old. In Zoroastrianism, guardian angels were called fravashis. Before Christianity, the Greeks had *daemons*, who were protective spirits. The Romans also had protective guardians; Roman men had a *genius* and women a *juno*.

The Bible contains a number of instances in which individuals were helped by an angel, presumably that person's guardian angel. An angel appeared to Hagar, the runaway servant girl, and told her to return to her mistress, Sarah. An angel helped Daniel interpret his dreams. God told Moses: "Mine angel shall go before thee" (Exodus 32:34). Raphael acted as Tobias' guardian angel in the Book of Tobit. An angel rescued St. Peter from prison. St. Paul wrote: "Are they not all ministering spirits [angels], sent forth to minister for them who shall be heirs of salvation?" (Hebrews 1:14). Psalm 91:11 reads: "For he shall give his angels charge over thee, to keep thee in all thy ways."

Jesus Christ confirmed the existence of guardian angels when he said: "Take heed that ye despise not one of these little ones; for I say unto you, That in Heaven their angels do always behold the face of my Father which is in Heaven" (Matthew 18:10). Origen, an early Christian theologian, believed that everyone has both a good and an evil angel. The good angel guides and protects the person, and the evil angel tempts him or her.

St. Thomas Aquinas believed everyone has a guardian angel. In Catholic belief, every person receives a guardian angel at birth to look after them and guide them through life.

Pope Pius XI (1857–1939) had such a strong faith in his guardian angel that he used him every time he had a potentially difficult situation. While praying to his guardian angel, he would ask his angel to speak to the guardian angels of everyone involved in the situation to ensure the best outcome for everyone concerned.

In the Roman Catholic Church, October 2 is the feast of guardian angels. Catholic children still learn:

> *Angel of God, my guardian dear*
> *To whom His love commits me here;*
> *Ever this day [or night] be at my side,*
> *To light and guard, to rule and guide.*

At one time, seventy nations were protected by their guardian angels, who were known as Ethnarchs. Unfortunately—with the exception of Michael, guardian angel of Israel—these angels misused their authority and became fallen angels.

In the Jewish Talmud, it is said that every Jew has eleven thousand guardian angels. Muslims have four guardian angels, known as hafaza. Two watch over their charges during the day, while the other two look after the night. These four angels are kept busy writing down their charges' good and bad deeds. These records will be used to assess each person on Judgment Day.

It is important to communicate with your guardian angel in good times as well as bad. Your guardian angel will provide you with peace of mind in times of sorrow and misfortune and will fill you with good ideas, positivity, and a desire to do good in the happy times.

In angelology, the Schemhamphora angels have been used as guardian angels for specific birth dates. Note that the names of some of these angels can vary in spelling. You may find more information on each guardian angel in its own entry.

Aries

> March 21–25: Vehuiah (Vehujah)
> March 26–30: Jelial
> March 31–April 4: Sitael (Sirael)
> April 5–9: Elemiah
> April 10–14: Mahasiah
> April 15–20: Lelahel

Taurus

> April 21–25: Achaiah
> April 26–30: Cahatel
> May 1–5: Haziel
> May 6–10: Aladiah
> May 11–15: Lauviah (also June 11–15) (Laviah)
> May 16–20: Hahaiah (also July 17–22) (Hahajah)

Gemini

May 21–25: Iezalel
May 26–31: Mebahel
June 1–5: Hariel
June 6–10: Hakamiah
June 11–15: Lauviah (also May 11–15) (Laviah)
June 16–21: Caliel

Cancer

June 22–26: Leuviah (Leviah)
June 27–July 1: Pahaliah
July 2–6: Nelchael (Nelakhel)
July 7–11: Ieiaeil (Jejalel)
July 12–16: Melahel
July 17–22: Hahajah (also May16–20) (Hahaiah)

Leo

July 23–27: Nith-Haiah (Nithhaja)
July 28–August 1: Haaiah
August 2–6: Terathel
August 7–12: Seheiah (Sehijah)
August 13–17: Reiiel (Rejajel)
August 18–22: Omael

Virgo

August 23–28: Lecabel
August 29–September 2: Vasiariah
September 3–7: Yehudiah
September 8–12: Lehahiah
September 13–17: Chavakiah
September 18–23: Menadel

Libra

September 24–28: Anael
September 29–October 3: Haamiah
October 4–8: Rehael

October 9–13: Ieiazel (Ihiazel)
October 14–18: Hahahel (Hahael)
October 19–23: Mikael

Scorpio

October 24–28: Veualiah (Vevaliah)
October 29–November 2: Ielahiah
November 3–7: Sealiah
November 8–12: Ariel
November 13–17: Asaliah
November 18–22: Mihael

Sagittarius

November 23–27: Vahuel (Vehael)
November 28–December 2: Daniel
December 3–7: Hahasiah
December 8–12: Imamiah
December 13–16: Nanael
December 17–21: Nithael

Capricorn

December 22–26: Mebahiah
December 27–31: Poiel (Polial)
January 1–5: Nemamiah
January 6–10: Ieilael (Ieliel)
January 11–15: Harahel
January 16–20: Mitzrael (Mizrael)

Aquarius

January 21–25: Umabel (Umbael)
January 26–30: Iahhel
January 31–February 4: Anauel
February 5–9: Mehiel
February 10–14: Damabiah
February 15–19: Manakel (Manadel)

Pisces
>February 20–24: Eiael
>February 25–29: Habuhiah (Habajuah)
>March 1–5: Rochel
>March 6–10: Gabamiah (Jabamiah)
>March 11–15: Haiaiel (Hajael)
>March 16–20: Mumiah (Mumijah)

See *Aquinas (St. Thomas)*, *Ethnarchs*, *fallen angels*, *fravashis*, *hafaza*, individual angels, *Michael*, *Raphael*, *Schemhamphoras*, *Zoroastrianism*.

Haaiah (Ha-ee-yah) **(Haajah):** Haaiah is a member of the Schemhamphoras, the seventy-two angels who have the names of God in Jewish scripture. Haaiah belongs to the choir of Dominions and promotes justice, civility, liberty, and morality. He is guardian angel for people born between July 28 and August 1.

See *Dominions, guardian angels, Schemhamphoras.*

Haamiah (Ha-ar-mee-yah)**:** Haamiah is the angel of integrity and a member of the order of Powers. He is also one of the seventy-two Schemhamphoras, a group of angels who bear the various names of God found in Jewish scriptures. Haamiah acts as a guardian angel to people born between September 29 and October 3. Haamiah traditionally looks after genuine seekers of spiritual knowledge. He also enjoys granting happiness to all long-lasting relationships.

See *guardian angels, Powers, Schemhamphoras.*

Habbiel (**Habiel**)**:** Habbiel lives in the First Heaven and looks after Monday, which is the day of the moon. Habbiel has a strong interest in love, loyalty, and commitment. He is the angel to call on if you or your partner experience problems in committing to each other. Habbiel helps people find the necessary trust and openness to commit to each other. Consequently, he is sometimes referred to as an angel of love. Habbiel's role also extends to loyalty and commitment in every area of life.

Habujah (Ha-bu-hee-yah) **(Habuhiah, Habuiah, or Chabuiah):** Habujah is a member of the Schemhamphoras, the seventy-two angels who have the names of God from Jewish scripture. He looks after fertility and agriculture. He is guardian angel for people born between February 25 and 29.

See *guardian angels, Schemhamphoras.*

Hadraniel (Hadariel or Hadriel): "Greatness of God." In Hebrew tradition, God rebuked Hadraniel because he blocked Moses' path and made Moses weep when he arrived in Heaven to receive the Torah. After this, Hadraniel decided to help Moses, which he did by using his powerful voice.

Apparently, Hadraniel's voice can penetrate two hundred thousand firmaments. Each word he says produces twelve thousand flashes of lightning. Hadraniel is more than two million miles tall. (Amazingly, Sandalphon is much taller, and actually dwarfs Hadraniel.) Hadraniel helps people increase the love they feel to their partners. You should call on Hadraniel whenever you need help to express yourself. It is possible that Hadraniel is also Adriel. Hadraniel is based at the entry to Heaven, and serves as one of God's gatekeeper angels.

See *Adriel, gatekeeper angels, Sandalphon.*

Hael: You should call upon Hael when you wish to send blessings to someone to thank them for their help or kindness.

Hafaza: The hafaza are the Islamic equivalent of the guardian angels. However, rather than having one guardian angel each, Muslims have four hafaza. Two keep a watchful eye on their charge during the day, while the other two look after them at night. One of their tasks is to protect the soul of their charge from the attacks of Satan and other evil spirits. They are better known, though, for recording their charge's good and bad deeds. The books these deeds are recorded in will be read on Judgment Day and will determine whether or not the person will be admitted into Heaven.

See *guardian angels*.

Hagar: In the Book of Genesis, Hagar was an Egyptian girl who was the handmaid, or servant, to Abraham's wife Sarah. The Angel of the Lord visited her on two occasions. The first time occurred when she had fled into the wilderness to escape the wrath of Sarah. The angel of the Lord told her she would give birth to a son, whom she should call Ishmael (Genesis 16:1–14). On the second occasion, she was again in the wilderness as Abraham had sent her away at his wife's request. She placed her infant son under a shrub and sat down far away so she would not see him die. God heard her crying and sent an angel to comfort her. This angel told her that Ishmael's seed would spawn a great nation (Genesis 21:14–19).

See *Lord (Angel of the)*.

Hagiel: Hagiel is an angel of the planet Venus and is frequently invoked by magicians when making talismans or performing spells relating to love and romance.

Hagith: Hagith is one of the Olympian spirits who rule over the 196 sections of Heaven. Hagith is responsible for twenty-one of these. Hagith also looks after the planet Venus. Hagith governed the world from 1410 to 1900 CE.

See *Olympian spirits*.

Hahahel (Ha-ha-hel): Hahahel is a member of the choir of Virtues and is also one of the seventy-two Schemhamphoras, a group of angels who bear the various names of God found in Jewish scriptures.

Hahahel is guardian angel of people born between October 14 and 18. He helps sick people regain their health and vitality.

See *guardian angels, Schemhamphoras, Virtues.*

Hahajah (Ha-ha-ee-yah) **(Hahaiah, Haheuiah, Hahuiah, or Mahuia):** Hahajah belongs to the choir of Cherubim and is also one of the seventy-two Schemhamphoras who bear the names of God from Jewish scripture. He is guardian angel of people born between May 16 and 20 and also of July 17 through 22. He is considered an angel of health and well-being, and also provides peace of mind for people who are in need of it.

See *Cherubim, guardian angels, Schemhamphoras.*

Hahasiah (Ha-ha-see-yah): Hahasiah is one of the seventy-two Schemhamphoras, a group of angels who bear the various names of God found in Jewish scriptures. He is also guardian angel of people born between December 3 and 7. Hahasiah helps people who are studying to retain what they have learned.

See *guardian angels, Schemhamphoras.*

Hajael (Ha-ee-ya-el) **(Haiaiel):** Hajael is one of the seventy-two Schemhamphoras, a group of angels who bear the various names of God found in Jewish scriptures. Hajael is the guardian angel of people born between March 11 and 15. He helps people understand complicated ideas and concepts.

See *guardian angels, Schemhamphoras.*

Hakamiah (Ha-kar-mee-yah): Hakamiah is a member of the choir of Cherubim and is considered the guardian angel of France. He is also one of the seventy-two Schemhamphoras, a group of angels who bear the various names of God found in Jewish scriptures. He is guardian angel of people born between June 6 and 10 and provides motivation and help for people who want to progress.

See *Cherubim, guardian angels, Schemhamphoras.*

Hamael: Hamael can be invoked whenever you need to appear calm and dignified. Hamael provides persistence, determination, and practicality.

Hamalatal-'Arsh: In Islam, the hamalatal-'arsh are the four throne-bearers who carry the chair of God. They appear as a man, a bull, an eagle, and a lion.

Hamaliel: Hamaliel is chief of the choir of Virtues and ruler of August. He is the Archangel who looks after people born under the zodiac sign of Virgo. Hamaliel can be invoked for any matters involving logic and attention to detail.
  See *Archangels, zodiac (angels of the)*.

Hamied: Hamied helps create miracles. You can call on him when you need a miracle in your life.

Hanael: See *Anael*.

Haniel: "Glory of God." Haniel is one of the rulers of the order of Principalities and is considered one of the ten main Archangels. He is a planetary angel and one of the rulers of the planet Venus. Francis Barrett, author of *The Magus*, wrote that Haniel was ruler of the choir of Innocents. Haniel is sometimes thought to be the angel who transported Enoch to Heaven.
  See *Archangels, Enoch, Innocents, planetary angels*.

Harahel (Ha-ra-hel) **(Harakel, Harael, Hararel, or Haroel):** Harahel is one of the seventy-two Schemhamphoras, a group of angels who bear the various names of God found in Jewish scriptures. He is the angel responsible for schools, universities, libraries, archives, and other repositories of knowledge. He can be called upon for help and advice on any matters involving study, learning, and examinations. Harahel acts as guardian angel for people born between January 11 and 15.
  See *guardian angels, Schemhamphoras*.

Harahil: In the Islamic tradition, Harahil is the angel who looks after dawn every day. He hangs a large white diamond over the eastern horizon. Sharahil, the angel who looks after the night, hangs a large black diamond over the western horizon. These two diamonds work together to ensure the proper rotation of the earth, and also that night follows day.

See *Sharahil.*

Harbonah: Harbonah is one of the leaders of the destroying angels. He is sometimes called the Angel of Annihilation.

See *destroying angels.*

Hariel (Ha-ree-el)**:** Hariel is a member of the choir of Cherubim and is one of the seventy-two Schemhamphoras, a group of angels who bear the various names of God found in Jewish scriptures. He has a strong interest in natural science. He is guardian angel of people born between June 1 and 5 and provides people with a sense of beauty and appreciation of the finer things in life.

See *Cherubim, guardian angels, Schemhamphoras.*

Harquaeel (Hark-yoo-a-eel)**:** Harquaeel is an angel in the Islamic tradition. He was created with eighteen thousand wings, and decided to use them to see how large God's throne was. God was pleased with this idea and gave Harquaeel another eighteen thousand wings to help him achieve this task. Harquaeel flew for three thousand light-years before he became tired and stopped to rest. God ordered him to carry on, and Harquaeel flew for another three thousand light-years. Again, he became tired and had to stop. God ordered him to keep on flying. Harquaeel flew for yet another three thousand light-years before he had to stop. He asked God how many times he had circled God's throne. God replied that in nine thousand light-years, Harquaeel had not reached even the first pillar in God's throne. Harquaeel felt devastated until God told him that even if he flew until the Day of Resurrection, he would not reach even the first pillar.

Harut (Haroth or Haroot): Harut and Marut are two Islamic angels who came down from Heaven to teach humans how to govern themselves. Unfortunately, they revealed the secret name of God to a human woman, who used this knowledge to visit the planet Venus. The two angels were punished for their transgressions, and are imprisoned, head downwards, in a pit near Babylon. They are considered fallen angels.

See *fallen angels, Marut.*

Hashmal (Chasmal): See *Hashmalin.*

Hashmalin: The Hashmalin are a choir of angels in the Jewish tradition. People have identified them with the Hayyoth, Seraphim, Cherubim, Powers, and Dominions. Their leader is Hashmal, who is often called the fire-speaking angel. Moses Maimonides listed them as fourth in importance in his hierarchy of angels. In the Zohar, they are sixth.

See *Cherubim, Dominions, Hayyoth, hierarchy of angels, Powers, Seraphim.*

Haurvatat (How-va-tat)**:** Haurvatat is an Amesha Spenta, one of the Archangels in Zoroastrianism. Haurvatat and Ameretat are usually regarded as sisters. Haurvatat is the angel of wholeness and perfection, and she rules over water.

See *Ameretat, Amesha Spentas, Archangels, Zoroastrianism.*

Havani: Havani is a yazata angel in Zoroastrianism who looks after the period between sunrise and noon every day.

See *yazata, Zoroastrianism.*

Hayyoth (Hay-yot) **(Chayyoth or Hayyot):** In the Jewish tradition, the Hayyoth are a group of Merkabah angels who live in the Seventh Heaven closest to God. They are angels of fire. Because of this, they are sometimes compared with the Cherubim in the Christian tradition. According to Jewish lore, Raziel has to spread his wings over the Hayyoth to ensure their fiery breath does not burn the other angels attending God's throne. The Hayyoth have four faces (human, lion, bull, and eagle), four huge wings, the feet of a calf, and the hands of a human. Moses Maimonides (1135–1203) listed them as the highest rank of angels in his hierarchy of angels. Their main tasks are to carry the throne of God and to sing his praises. The leader of the Hayyoth is Chayyiel.

See *Chayyiel, Cherubim, hierarchy of angels, Merkabah.*

Haziel (Hay-zee-el): "Vision of God." Haziel is a member of the choir of Cherubim and is one of the seventy-two Schemhamphoras who bear the names of God from Jewish scripture. Haziel is the guardian angel for people born between May 1 and 5. He should be invoked whenever you are seeking God's mercy and compassion, or are seeking harmony between groups of people.

See *Cherubim, guardian angels, Schemhamphoras.*

Heavenly Host: "Heavenly host" is a term that covers all the angels in Heaven. Not surprisingly, many of the heavenly host came to welcome the birth of Jesus: "And suddenly there was with the angel a multitude of the heavenly host praising God, and saying, Glory to God in the highest, and on earth peace, good will toward men" (Luke 2:13–14). In Heaven, the host stand on the right- and left-hand sides of God: "I saw the Lord sitting on his throne, and all the host of Heaven standing by him on his right hand and on his left" (1 Kings 22:19).

Heavens: Christians, Jews, and Muslims all believe in Heaven. Apocalyptic accounts of Heaven range from one Heaven to ten, but most agree on seven, probably because of the seven visible planets. The tradition of seven Heavens probably originated in Mesopotamia seven thousand years ago.

First Heaven: The First Heaven is called *Vilon* from the Latin word *velum*, which means "veil." It contains the physical world. It is ruled by Gabriel and is home to all the angels connected with the natural phenomena of the universe.

Second Heaven: The Second Heaven is called *Raqia*, meaning "expanse." It is ruled by Raphael. Some authorities believe Raphael and Zachariel share the task of ruling the Second Heaven. The Second Heaven is the home of sinners who are waiting for Judgment Day. Some of the fallen angels are held here, too. In the Islamic tradition, the Second Heaven is the home of Jesus and John the Baptist.

Third Heaven: The Third Heaven is called *Shechakim* or *Shehaqim*, which means "the sky." Baradiel is in charge of the Third Heaven. (The Sixth and Seventh Books of Moses say Anahel rules the Third Heaven.) The southern half of this Heaven contains the Garden of Eden and the Tree of Life. Three hundred angels of light protect them. The northern half of the Third Heaven could not be more different, as it contains Hell. Not surprisingly, some of the fallen angels are held here.

Fourth Heaven: The Fourth Heaven is called *Zebhul*, meaning "the lofty place." It is ruled by Michael. It contains the Holy Temple and the Altar of God.

Fifth Heaven: The Fifth Heaven is called *Machon*, which means "the dwelling." Most sources say that Zadkiel rules the Fifth Heaven. (Some accounts give this task to Sandalphon.) Some of the fallen angels are held here (as well as in the Second and Third Heavens).

Sixth Heaven: The Sixth Heaven is called *Makon*, meaning "the habitation." Zebul rules the Sixth Heaven at night, and Sabath rules during the daytime hours. All the celestial records are kept here, and choirs of angels endlessly study them.

Seventh Heaven: The Seventh Heaven is called *Araboth*, meaning "the clouds." Archangel Cassiel rules the Seventh Heaven. God, the Seraphim, Cherubim, and the Thrones live here. Human souls waiting to be born also live here.

See *Anahel, Baradiel, Cassiel, Cherubim,* individual angels, *Sabath, Sandalphon, Seraphim, Thrones, Zadkiel, Zebul.*

Hemah: According to Jewish legend, Hemah is one of the destroying angels. He is also the angel of death for domestic animals. Legend says he tried to kill Moses by swallowing him but failed because God saw what was happening. God made Hemah regurgitate Moses, and then, rather surprisingly, gave Moses permission to kill Hemah. In the Zohar, Hemah, Af, and Mashit are the three demons who punish people who commit idolatry, incest, or murder.

See *Af, death (angel of), destroying angels, Mashit.*

Heman: Heman, Asaph, and Jeduthun are the choir directors of the angels who continually praise God. Heman directs the choir in the morning, Jeduthun takes over in the evening, and Asaph looks after the night. Jehoel, at least in the Jewish tradition, is believed to be the director in chief. Heman and Jeduthun are mentioned by name in the annotations to some of the Psalms. This appears to indicate that they were in charge of the music at the Temple of Jerusalem and were promoted to angels because of their talents. Heman is mentioned at the start of Psalm 88: "A Song or Psalm for the sons of Korah, to the Chief Musician upon Mahalath Leannoth, Maschil of Heman, the Ezrahite."

See *Asaph, Jeduthon, Jehoel.*

Hierarchy of Angels: The Bible mentions nine groups of angels, but does not give any indication as to their ranking. Consequently, over the years, many theologians and religious scholars have come up with their own suggestions. By far the best known of these is the one by Dionysius the Areopagite, who gave us the term "hierarchy." Dionysius was at one time thought to be the Dionysius mentioned in the Acts of the Apostles who was converted to Christianity by St. Paul (Acts 17:34) and became the first Christian bishop of Athens. However, Pseudo-Dionysius, as this author is often called, wrote his book, *The Celestial Hierar-*

chy, in the early sixth century. Presumably, Dionysius, who was possibly a Syrian monk, adopted this pseudonym hoping it would give his book more credibility. If this was his aim, it succeeded, and his hierarchy was adopted by the Catholic Church. Dionysius' hierarchy gained even more credibility when St. Thomas Aquinas (1225–1274), the Italian theologian who is frequently called "the angelic doctor," adopted it seven hundred years later. Other eminent theologians, including Alan of Lille, St. Bonaventure, John Duns Scotus, Hugh of St. Victor, and Thomas Gallus also wrote commentaries on Dionysius' work. His hierarchy is still considered the most important classification of angels today.

Dionysius divided the angelic hosts into nine groups or choirs.

1. Seraphim
2. Cherubim
3. Thrones
4. Dominions
5. Virtues
6. Powers
7. Principalities
8. Archangels
9. Angels

The choirs are grouped into three orders: The first order contains the Seraphim, Cherubim, and Thrones, the angels closest to God. The second order contains the princes or leaders of the heavenly kingdom—the Dominions, Virtues, and Powers. The third order contains the ministering angels—the Principalities, Archangels, and Angels.

Dionysius obtained the names of these choirs from the Bible. The Seraphim and Cherubim were mentioned in the Old Testament (Genesis 3:24; Isaiah 6:2). He considered these to be closest to God. The other names came from the writings of St. Paul in the New Testament (Colossians 1:16; Ephesians 1:21). Dionysius believed there were seven Archangels: Chamuel, Gabriel, Jophiel, Michael, Raphael, Uriel, and Zadkiel.

Other hierarchies have been suggested. In Dante Alighieri's (1265–1321) *The Divine Comedy* he switched the places of the Archangels and Principalities, but otherwise kept to Dionysius' arrangement. *The Apostolic Constitutions* predates Dionysius and lists ten choirs. It adds aeons and hosts, but does not include Dominions. Other creators of angel hierarchies include: St. Ambrose, St. Jerome, St. Gregory the Great, St. Isidore of Seville, St. John Damascene, Rudolf Steiner, and Billy Graham.

Rudolf Steiner's hierarchy is:

1. Spirits of Love (corresponding with Seraphim)
2. Spirits of the Harmonies (Cherubim)
3. Spirits of Will (Thrones)
4. Spirits of Wisdom (Dominions)
5. Spirits of Movement (Virtues)
6. Spirits of Form (Powers)
7. Spirits of Personality or Time (Principalities)
8. Fire-Spirits (Archangels)
9. Sons of Life or of Twilight (Angels)

In the Jewish tradition, there are two main hierarchies. Moses Maimonides (1135–1203) suggested:

1. Hayyot (Hayyoth)
2. Ophanim
3. Erelim
4. Hashmalin
5. Seraphim
6. Malakhim
7. Elohim
8. Bene Elohim
9. Cherubim
10. Ishim

The Zohar (c.1275 CE) listed the angels as:

1. Malakhim
2. Erelim
3. Seraphim
4. Hayyot (Hayyoth)
5. Ophanim
6. Hashmalin
7. Elim
8. Elohim
9. Bene Elohim
10. Ishim

Alan of Lille also created an Exordo, or hierarchy of the fallen angels.

John Calvin (1509–1564), founder of the Presbyterian Church, had no time for hierarchies of angels. He wrote that conversations on this subject were "the vain babblings of idle men."

See *aeons, Alan of Lille, Angels, Aquinas (St. Thomas), Archangels, Bene Elohim, Bonaventure (Saint), Chamuel, Cherubim, Dionysius the Areopagite, Dominions, Elim, Elohim, Erelim, Exordo, fallen angels, Gabriel, Hashmalin, Hayyoth, Ishim, Jophiel, Malakhim, Michael, Ophanim, Powers, Principalities, Raphael, Scotus (John Duns), Seraphim, Steiner (Rudolf), Thrones, Uriel, Virtues, Zadkiel.*

Hinduism, Angels of: Hindus believe in a Universal Soul called Brahman who is present in everything. All other deities in their pantheon are aspects of Brahman. Although there are no official angels in Hinduism, they have Devas, or "shining ones," who are winged beings that help people. The Devas are helped by Gandharvas, who are usually depicted with wings. When the mother of Buddha conceived, she was taken to the Himalayas by four guardian angels and protected by four sword-carrying angels.

See *guardian angels.*

Hizkiel: According to the Zohar, Hizkiel and Kafziel are Archangel Gabriel's chief assistants in times of war.

See *Archangels, Gabriel, Kafziel.*

Hodniel: Hodniel is one of the angels who can be called upon to help cure human stupidity.

Hodson, Geoffrey: Geoffrey Hodson (1886–1983), a gifted clairvoyant and Theosophist, was contacted by an angel called Bethelda in 1924 while sitting on a hillside in Gloucestershire, England. While he was meditating, the sky was suddenly filled with light, and Geoffrey's consciousness was taken over by an incredible radiant light. He became aware of a Heavenly being who harmonized its mind with his. This was Bethelda. In his book, *The Brotherhood of Angels and Men* (1927), Geoffrey Hodson recorded the seven groups of angels that Bethelda taught him:

1. Angels of Power. These angels help people develop spiritually.
2. Angels of Healing. These angels help people maintain good health.
3. Guardian angels of the Home. These angels protect the home.
4. Building Angels. These are inspirational angels who help people aspire to be all they can be in the areas of mind, body, and spirit.
5. Angels of Nature. These are the elemental spirits, sometimes called devas. They live in fire, earth, air, and water.
6. Angels of Music. These angels sing God's praises and inspire people to sing and worship God.
7. Angels of Beauty and Art. These angels inspire and motivate people involved in creative activities. They also help people appreciate beauty in all its forms.

Geoffrey Hodson saw angels and humankind as two branches of God's family. He taught that we should work more closely with the angelic kingdom, as this connection would help our spiritual development.

See *Bethelda*.

Holy Immortals: See *Amesha Spentas*.

Hru: Hru, according to the teachings of the Hermetic Order of the Golden Dawn, is the angel in charge of all Secret Wisdom. Some tarot card readers call on Hru for help and guidance when making their prognostications.

Huris: Huris are dark-eyed, sensuous, and incredibly beautiful female angels in the Islamic tradition. They provide pleasure to people who have earned eternal happiness by their good deeds on earth. Every new arrival to Heaven is, as long as he merits it, provided with seventy-two huris who exist solely to satisfy his every desire. The huris become virgins again at the end of every night.

Hvare-Khshaeta (Hah-reh Shah-et-eh): "Shining Sun." Hvare-Khshaeta is a yazata angel in Zoroastrianism who rules over the sun. Maonghah rules over the moon.

See *Maonghah, yazata, Zoroastrianism*.

I AM: I AM is one of the most important of the Enochian angels. In fact, it is possible that she is a supreme being in this system, taking a similar role to that of the Shekinah in Judaism. I AM is the mother of Madimi, another important Enochian angel.

See *Enochian angels, Madimi, Shekinah*.

Iachadiel (Ee-ak-ad-yee-el): Iachadiel is one of the angels of the moon and is sometimes invoked by magicians when performing rituals involving the moon.

Iahhel (Ee-ah-hel) **(Iahel):** Iahhel looks after the needs of hermits, philosophers, teachers, and anyone who is studying. He is a peace-loving angel who can be invoked for help in meditation, and for counsel during periods of self-imposed retirement from the world. Iahhel is one of the seventy-two Schemhamphoras, a group of angels who bear the various names of God found in Jewish scriptures. Iahhel is also the guardian angel of people born between January 26 and 30.

See *guardian angels, Schemhamphoras*.

Ialdaboath (Ee-ald-a-bo-at) **(Iadalbaoth or Jaldaboath):** In Gnosticism, Ialdaboath is one of the seven archons and is sometimes considered their leader. He is often considered to be the son of Sophia. In the First Book of Enoch, he is associated with Samael, a fallen angel.

See *archons, fallen angels, Samael, Sophia.*

Iblis (Eblis): In Islam, Iblis is Satan, or "the enemy." After God created Adam, God asked all the angels to bow down to him. Iblis refused, and God cursed him until the Day of Doom. However, as this punishment has been delayed until Judgment Day, Iblis is free to entice people away from God. Iblis refused to prostrate himself before Adam because Iblis himself had been made of fire, while Adam had been created from mud.

See *Satan.*

Ielahiah (Yay-lah-hee-yah) **(Jelabiah or Yelaiah):** Ielahiah is one of the seventy-two Schemhamphoras, a group of angels who bear the various names of God found in Jewish scriptures. He assists people involved in matters of justice. He is guardian angel of people born between October 29 and November 2 and encourages people to participate in their local community to make it a better place.

See *guardian angels, Schemhamphoras.*

Ieliel (Yay-lee-el) **(Ieilael or Yeiael):** Ieliel is one of the seventy-two Schemhamphoras, a group of angels who bear the various names of God found in Jewish scriptures. Ieliel is guardian angel of people born between January 6 and 10. He helps people pay attention to details.

See *guardian angels, Schemhamphoras.*

Iezalel (Yay-zar-lee-el): Iezalel is guardian angel of people born between May 21 and 25. He helps people communicate more effectively and has a strong interest in home and family life. It is possible that Iezalel is Jajajel.

See *guardian angels, Jajajel.*

Ihiazel (Jejazel): Ihiazel is one of the seventy-two Schemhamphoras, a group of angels who bear the various names of God found in Jewish scriptures. Ihiazel is also guardian angel of people born between October 9 and 13. He helps people gain confidence in themselves and their abilities.

See *guardian angels, Schemhamphoras.*

Imamiah (Ee-ma-mee-yah): Imamiah is, or was, one of the seventy-two Schemhamphoras, a group of angels who bear the various names of God found in Jewish scriptures. However, he may have been demoted, as one story describes him as a fallen angel. Imamiah is guardian angel of people born between December 8 and 12. People who want to become more popular or feel more at ease around others can call upon Imamiah for help.

See *fallen angels, guardian angels, Schemhamphoras.*

Inias: At the Council of Rome in 745 CE, a number of angels were removed from the list of honored angels because the church leaders were concerned about the huge amount of public interest in angels. These angels, known as reprobated angels, were: Adimus, Inias, Raguel, Sabaoc, Simiel, Tubuas, and Archangel Uriel. Inias was so upset at his relegation that he began interrupting lengthy sermons with noisy and extremely unpleasant bursts of flatulence.

See *reprobated angels,* individual angels.

Innocents: According to Francis Barrett, author of *The Magus,* the Innocents were an order of angels. In his hierarchy of angels, the Innocents ranked tenth and were ruled by Haniel.

See *Haniel, hierarchy of angels.*

Iofiel: See *Jophiel.*

Irin, The (Irrin): The Irin are twin angels who, along with their fellow twins, the qaddism, adjudicate on God's behalf at the Heavenly Court. They are said to be more important than Metatron.

Enoch confirms this in the Third Book of Enoch by saying: "Each one of them is equal to all the rest put together."

See *Metatron*, *qaddism*.

Isda: Isda is the angel of physical, emotional, and spiritual nourishment. Because of the connection to physical nourishment, Isda is also sometimes called the angel of food.

Ishim (Issim, Ischim, or Izachim): The Ishim are the lowest-ranked angels in the Jewish hierarchy of angels compiled by Moses Maimonides. The hierarchy listed in the Zohar also places them in this position. They are made of fire and ice and live in the Fifth Heaven, where their main role is to praise God.

See *hierarchy of angels*.

Islam, Angels of: Angels are mentioned more than eighty times in the Koran. In Islamic belief, angels praise God and act as his messengers. They often act on God's behalf in matters concerning humanity. Angels are also involved in the period between a person's death and the resurrection. Every person has four guardian angels—two for the daytime and two for the night. In Islam, angels are created from light. They possess gender, but do not reproduce. Because they lack free will, they cannot sin, and instead obediently carry out all of Allah's orders (Sura 66:6). Islamic angels have two, three, or four pairs of wings.

There are four Archangels in Islam: Djibril (Gabriel), Mikhail (Michael), Azrael, and Israfel. Djibril and Mikhail are mentioned by name in the Koran. Azrael (Izra'il) is the angel of death, and Israfel the angel of music. There are also other ranks of angels: the abdals (seventy angels who ensure the universe unfolds in the way it should), the El-Karubiyan (Cherubim), the hafaza (guardian angels), the huris (female angels who live in Heaven), the al-zabaniya (the nineteen guardians of Hell), and the malaika (angels who record mankind's good and bad deeds).

The devil in Islam is called Iblis. He is also known as *al-shay-ton*, which means "the Satan." He is a fallen angel in Islamic belief because he refused to bow down before Adam (Sura 15:30–33). Iblis was guilty of both pride and disobedience. Because of this, Allah sentenced him to damnation, but the punishment has been delayed until Judgment Day.

There are two other angels who cannot be compared with angels in Judaism or Christianity: Munkar and Nakir. They are black and have blue eyes. Their task is to question people in their graves to determine the strength of their faith.

See *Archangels, Cherubim, El-Karubiyan, fallen angels, guardian angels, hafaza, huris, Iblis,* individual angels, *malaika.*

Israel: Authorities differ as to which choir of angels Israel belongs to. He has been called a Throne, a Hayyoth, and an Archangel. Israel has also been associated with Israel-Jacob, which is a mysterious combination of Jacob, father of the people of Israel, and the angel he wrestled with for a whole night. While they were fighting, the angel said: "Thy name shall be called no more Jacob, but Israel" (Genesis 32:28).

See *Archangels, Hayyoth, Thrones.*

Israfil (Israfel or Asrafil): In the Islamic tradition, Israfil is the Archangel who will blow the trumpet on the Day of Judgment. Because of his association with a trumpet, Israfil is often called the angel of music. Israfil kept Muhammad company for three years, until he was replaced by Djibril, God's messenger. Israfil gazes into Hell three times each day and three times each night. The earth is watered by the tears Israfil sheds after gazing into Hell. Fortunately, Allah quells the tears before Israfil can flood the entire earth. Israfil is an immensely tall angel with many mouths and tongues. He uses his mouths to glorify God in one thousand languages. He is said to have the sweetest speaking voice of any of God's creation. He has four wings and is covered with hair.

Edgar Allan Poe (1809–1849) wrote a poem titled *Israfel*, which begins:

> In Heaven a spirit doth dwell
>> "Whose heart-strings are a lute";
> None sing so wildly well
> As the angel Israfel,
> And the giddy stars (so legends tell)
> Ceasing their hymns, attend the spell
>> Of his voice, all mute.

See *Archangels, Djibril.*

Itqal: Itqal works with Archangel Haniel, and specializes in resolving disagreements, especially between family members. Itqal also restores love, affection, and enhances consideration of others.
See *Archangels, Haniel.*

Izad: The Izads are an order of angel in Zoroastrianism. They relate to the Christian Cherubim and are charged with protecting the peace, happiness, and innocence of the world. There are twenty-eight members of this order, and they constantly surround and worship Ahura Mazda. The chief of this order is believed to be Mithra.
See *Ahura Mazda, Cherubim, Mithra, Zoroastrianism.*

Izrael: See *Azrael.*

Jabamiah (Yar-ba-mee-yah) **(Gagamiah):** Jabamiah assists Archangel Uriel in his work. He is one of the seventy-two Schemhamphoras, a group of angels who bear the various names of God found in Jewish scriptures. He is also guardian angel of people born between March 6 and 10. He helps people pursue their goals.

See *Archangels, guardian angels, Schemhamphoras, Uriel.*

Jael: Jael belongs to the choir of Cherubim. Depictions of him (and Zarall, another Cherub) were carved into the Ark of the Covenant. The Bible says: "And thou shalt make two cherubims of gold, of beaten work shalt they make them, in the two ends of the mercy seat. And make one cherub on the one end, and the other cherub on the other end: even of the mercy seat shall ye make the cherubims on the two ends thereof. And the cherubims shall stretch forth their wings on high, covering the mercy seat with their wings, and their faces shall look one to another; toward the mercy seat shall the faces of the cherubims be" (Exodus 25:18–20). Jael may be the same angel as Jaoel.

See *Ark of the Covenant, Cherubim, Jaoel, Zarall.*

Jajajel (Yay-yay-yel): Jajajel is one of the seventy-two Schemham-phoras, a group of angels who bear the various names of God found in Jewish scriptures. It is possible that Jajajel is Iezalel.

See *Iezalel, Schemhamphoras.*

Jaluha: Jaluha is a Gnostic angel who hands the cup of oblivion to the souls of sinners. After drinking from it, the humans forget the sinful deeds they performed while they were alive.

Jaoel: Jaoel is mentioned in the Apocalypse of Abraham 10:8 as one of God's most special angels, as he possessed God's "ineffable name." It is likely he is the angel better known as Jael.

See *Jael.*

Jarahel (Jareahel, Jevanael, or Levanael): In the Jewish Kabbalah, Jarahel is the angel responsible for the moon.

Jazeriel (Jareriel): Jazeriel is one of the twenty-eight angels who govern the mansions of the moon. Jazeriel is responsible for Alhaire, the thirteenth mansion. Jazeriel is a beneficial angel and helps harvests, journeys, and profit. He also helps prisoners gain their freedom.

See *mansions of the moon.*

Jeduthun: Jeduthun, Asaph, and Heman are the directors of the choirs of angels that continually praise God. Heman directs the choir in the morning, Jeduthun takes over in the evening, and Asaph looks after the night. Jehoel, at least in the Jewish tradition, is believed to be the director in chief. Jeduthun and Heman are mentioned by name in the annotations to some of the Psalms. This appears to indicate that they were in charge of the music at the Temple of Jerusalem, and were promoted to angels because of their talents. Jeduthun is mentioned at the start of Psalms 39, 62, and 77: "To the chief musician, to Jeduthun."

See *Asaph, Heman, Jehoel.*

Jegudiel: "The Glory of God." The Archangel Jegudiel helps anyone who is attempting to form a closer relationship with God. He provides opportunities for people who are honest, sincere, and prepared to work hard to achieve worthwhile spiritual goals.

Jehoel (Jahoel, Jaoel, or Yahoel): Jehoel is an Angel of the Presence, member of the Sarim, and ruler of the order of Seraphim. According to the Apocalypse of Abraham, Jehoel took Abraham on a tour of Heaven and ultimately took him to meet God. He is described as wearing purple robes and a rainbow-colored turban. His hair is white and his skin like sapphire. In Jewish legend, Jehoel leads the choirs that ceaselessly sing God's praises. Consequently, he holds a higher position than the other three choirmasters in Heaven: Asaph, Heman, and Jeduthun. Jehoel is happy to help musicians, especially singers.

See *Asaph, Heman, Jeduthun, Presence (Angels of the), Sarim, Seraphim.*

Jehudiel: Jehudiel is responsible for the movements of the planets. He is sometimes considered an Archangel.

See *Archangels.*

Jehuvajah (Yay-hoo-vah-yah): Jehuvajah is one of the seventy-two Schemhamphoras, a group of angels who bear the various names of God found in Jewish scriptures.

See *Schemhamphoras.*

Jejalel (Yay-yah-zel) **(Ieiaiel or Jehalel):** Jejalel is one of the seventy-two Schemhamphoras, a group of angels who bear the various names of God found in Jewish scriptures. He is the guardian angel of people born between July 7 and 11. He helps self-employed people make sound business decisions.

See *guardian angels, Schemhamphoras.*

Jelial (Jay-lee-al) **(Jeliel):** Jelial belongs to the order of Seraphim. Members of this choir do not normally assist people, as they are fully occupied serving God; however, Jelial has always had an interest in stimulating love and passion within existing relationships. You should call on Jelial if your relationship is suffering from a lack of passion. Jelial is also the guardian angel of Turkey and of people born between March 26 and 30.

See *guardian angels, Seraphim.*

Jeqon (Jay-kon)**:** Jeqon is one of the leaders of the Grigori. He brought the other angels down to earth to sleep with human women.

See *Grigori.*

Jerathel: Jerathel is one of the seventy-two Schemhamphoras, a group of angels who bear the various names of God found in Jewish scriptures.

See *Schemhamphoras.*

Jeremiel: "God's Mercy" Archangel Jeremiel is mentioned in the Book of Esdras and the First Book of Enoch. It is possible that Jeremiel is another name for Remiel or Archangel Uriel.

See *Archangels, Remiel, Uriel.*

Jesus: Angels played an important role at every stage of Jesus' life. Before his birth, Archangel Gabriel visited the Virgin Mary to tell her she was going to conceive (Luke 1:26–38). An "Angel of the Lord" visited Joseph, Mary's husband, and told him the child would be called "Jesus" (Matthew 1:18–25). Angels told the shepherds in the fields about the birth of Jesus (Luke 2:8–13). Angels came and ministered to Jesus after Satan tempted him during his forty days and forty nights in the wilderness (Matthew 4:11; Mark 1:13). During this time, Satan suggested Jesus jump off the pinnacle of the temple by saying: "If thou be the Son of God, cast thyself down: for it is written, He shall give His angels charge concerning Thee: and in their hands they shall bear thee up, lest at any time thou dash thy foot against a stone" (Matthew 4:5–6). An angel gave strength to Jesus when he prayed in the Garden of Gethsemane before his arrest (Luke 22:43). When Jesus was arrested, he said that if he prayed to his Father "he should presently give me more than twelve legions of angels" (Matthew 26:53). All four gospels tell how angels proclaimed the resurrection of Christ (Matthew 28:2–7; Mark 16:5; Luke 24:4–7; John 20:11–12). Angels will accompany Jesus at his Second Coming (Matthew 25:31; Mark 13:26–27).

Angels were also involved in the lives of people close to Jesus. Archangel Gabriel appeared to Zacharias and told him he would have a son named John (Luke 1:11–20). This baby grew up to become John the Baptist. An angel appeared to Joseph in a dream and told him to flee to Egypt, as King Herod wanted to kill Jesus (Matthew 2:13). An angel appeared again to tell Joseph when it was safe to return home to Israel (Matthew 2:19–21).

See *Archangels, Gabriel, Satan.*

Jezalel (Ieazel or Jezazel): Jezalel is one of the seventy-two Schemhamphoras, a group of angels who bear the various names of God found in Jewish scriptures.

See *Schemhamphoras.*

Jibril: See *Djibril.*

Joel: Joel is the Archangel who, according to the Book of Adam and Eve, led the first couple through the Garden of Eden and asked Adam to name everything he saw. This is a slightly different story than the one in the Bible: "And out of the ground the Lord God formed every beast of the field, and every fowl of the air; and brought them unto Adam to see what he would call them: and whatsoever Adam called every living creature, that was the name thereof" (Genesis 2:19).

See *Archangels.*

Jophiel (Johiel, Iophiel, Iofiel, or Zophiel): "The Beauty of God." Jophiel is one of the seven main Archangels, a member of the Sarim, and ruler of the order of Thrones. Some sources say he is one of the leaders of the Cherubim. Jophiel is believed to have guarded the Tree of Knowledge in the Garden of Eden. According to legend, it was Jophiel who expelled Adam and Eve from the Garden of Eden. He also looked after Noah's three sons. Jophiel is one of the Angels of the Presence, and he is believed to be a close friend of Metatron. He has a strong interest in beauty, and can be invoked by anyone involved in creating beauty in any form. You should call on him whenever you need help with a creative project. Jophiel is also the patron angel of artists and anyone engaged in creative activity.

See *Archangels, Cherubim, Metatron, Presence (Angels of the), Thrones, Yophiel.*

Kabbalah, Angels of the: The Kabbalah is an ancient Jewish mystical tradition. According to legend, Archangel Raziel taught the Kabbalah to Adam, and it was passed on by word of mouth until the twelfth century, when a collection of writings became edited into the first important Kabbalistic book, the Bahir. This book taught that the aim of mankind was to become fully united with the divine. The Kaballah teaches that God created the world as he wanted to see it. His creation is depicted in the Tree of Life. The world was created as a series of emanations, known as sephiroth. There are ten of these on the Tree of Life, connected by twenty paths.

In the Jewish tradition, there are ten orders of angels that relate to the ten sephiroth on the Tree of Life:

Chaioth ha-Qodesh ("Holy Living Beings") are considered the most important. They carry the throne of God.

Auphanim ("Wheels") have thousands of eyes and are considered the angels of wisdom. They appear as wheels within wheels.

Aralim ("Mighty Ones") are the angels of understanding.

Chashmalin ("Shining Ones") are the angels of mercy.

Seraphim ("Burning Ones") are the angels of justice and severity.

Malekim ("Kings") are the angels of beauty and harmony.

Tarshishim ("Sparkling Ones") are the angels of victory.

Bene Elohim ("Children of the Divine") are the angels of
glory.

Kerubim (Kerubeem) ("Strong Ones") have four wings and
four faces. They look after the universe.

Ishim ("Human Beings") look after the material world.

In the Kabbalah, Archangels are considered separately, as they
are over and above all the other angels. There are ten Archangels
in the Tree of Life:

Kether (Crown): Metatron

Chokmah (Wisdom): Raziel

Binah (Understanding): Tzaphiel

Chesed (Mercy): Zadkiel

Geburah (Severity): Samael (Khamael)

Tiphareth (Beauty): Michael

Netzach (Victory): Haniel

Hod (Glory): Raphael

Yesod (Foundation): Gabriel

Malkuth (Kingdom): Sandalphon

See *Adam, Archangels, Bene Elohim,* individual angels, *Ishim,
Kerubeem, Seraphim, Tarshishim.*

Kadishim: See *Qaddism.*

Kafziel: In the Jewish tradition, Kafziel is the angel of death for kings
and other important people. In the Zohar, Kafziel and Hizkiel act
as aides to Archangel Gabriel in times of war.
See *Archangels, death (angel of), Gabriel, Hizkiel.*

Kakabel (Kochbiel, Kokabel, or Kokabiel): "Star of God." Kaka-bel is a controversial angel who performs the honorable task of looking after the moon and stars. However, according to some accounts, he lost his reputation by teaching humans astrology. Even worse, in the First Book of Enoch, he was accused of mating with human women. Despite this, he still looks after astrologers, as well as the stars and their formations.

Kalka'il (Kal-ka-eel): In the Islamic tradition, Kalka'il is in charge of the huris in Heaven. He lives in the Fifth Heaven in Paradise.
    See *huris*.

Kasbeel (Kasbel): Kasbeel was originally called Beqa, which means "virtuous." However, he tried to trick Archangel Michael into telling him the secret name of God. Because of this, he became a fallen angel and his name was changed to Kasbeel, which means "deceiver." According to the First Book of Enoch, he is one of the leaders of the Grigori.
    See *Archangels, fallen angels, Grigori, Michael*.

Kasdeja (Kas-day-yah): Kasdeja is one of the Grigori, angels who came down to earth and slept with human women.
    See *Grigori*.

Kerubeem (Kerubim): Kerubeem is the Islamic equivalent of the Cherubim. According to legend, the Kerubeem were created from the tears of Mikhail. Their task is to endlessly praise God.
    See *Cherubim, Mikhail*.

Kerubiel (Kerubiel YHWH or Cherubiel): Kerubiel is one of the leaders of the Cherubim. His height spans all seven Heavens and powerful flames come out of his mouth with every word he speaks. His body consists of burning coals, covered with thousands of piercing eyes. Thunder, lightning, and earthquakes accompany him everywhere he goes. Despite his threatening appearance, he

glows with the divine light of the Shekinah, the feminine aspect
of God.

See *Cherubim, Shekinah.*

Kesef (Kezef): Kesef is one of the destroying angels. According to
Jewish legend, he led an attack on Moses at Mount Horeb. He
was captured by Aaron, the high priest, and imprisoned in the
Holy Tabernacle. During the time of his imprisonment, all death
on earth ceased. In the Jewish tradition, Kesef is considered an
angel of death.

See *death (angel of), destroying angels.*

Kether: Kether is one of the ten angels who rule over the holy sephiroth.

See *Kabbalah (angels of the).*

Khamael: In the Kabbalah, Khamael is considered the Archangel of
Geburah.

See *Archangels.*

Khshathra Vairya (Kish-ar-thra Vry-ah): Khshathra Vairya is an
Amesha Spenta, or Archangel, in Zoroastrianism who looks after
soldiers and people who are poor. His task is to bring prosperity
and knowledge of God to people who need it.

See *Amesha Spentas, Archangels, Zoroastrianism.*

Kokabel (Kokbiel, Kokabiel, or Kakabel): "Star of God." Kokabel
has the enormous task of looking after all the stars. Fortunately, he
has 365,000 angels at his disposal to help him. (However, according to the Third Book of Enoch, Kokabel—as Kokbiel—is one of
the Rulers of the Earth and is responsible for the planets.) To complicate matters, in the First Book of Enoch, Kokabel is described as
a fallen angel and part of the Grigori. Because of his involvement
with the stars, Kokabel is believed to be a highly skilled astrologer.

See *fallen angels, Grigori, Rulers of the Earth.*

Kokbiel: See *Kokabel*.

Kolazonta (Kolozanta): "The Chastiser." Kolazonta is an angel of destruction who threatened to destroy the Israelites when they were travelling through the wilderness. Aaron defeated him by purifying the Israeli camp.

Kutiel: Kutiel is an angel who offers help to anyone who dowses (or divines) for water, oil, gold, or anything else.

Kyriel (Kuriel): Kyriel is one of the twenty-eight angels who govern the mansions of the moon. He is responsible for Abnahaya, the twentieth mansion. In this role, he helps people tame wild animals, strengthens prisons, and has the ability to summon people to any place he cares to name. He also actively destroys the wealth of society.

As Kuriel, he is one of the many angels who guard and protect the gates of the West Wind.

See *mansions of the moon*.

Labbiel: Labbiel was Archangel Raphael's original name. God changed his name to Raphael when the angel supported God's concept of creating humankind.

See *Archangels, Raphael*.

Lahabiel: Lahabiel is one of Raphael's chief assistants. He can be invoked to ward off evil of any sort. Traditionally, Lahabiel was invoked to protect people from magic spells, curses, or the evil eye, but he can be invoked whenever you see evil in any form. His name is often inscribed on protective amulets.

See *Raphael*.

Lahash: In Jewish legend, Lahash and Zakun are powerful angels who led 184 myriads of angels who seized the prayers of Moses' followers when they asked God to let Moses live long enough to reach the Promised Land. This prevented any of the prayers from reaching God. Lahash apparently had second thoughts about the seizure and tried to restore some of the prayers, but Samael heard of this and bound Lahash with chains of fire. He took him to God "where he received sixty blows of fire and was expelled from the inner chamber of God because, contrary to God's wish, he had attempted to aid Moses in the fulfilment of his desire" (Louis Ginzberg, *Legends of the Jews*, 809). As a result of his actions, Lahash is considered a fallen angel.

See *fallen angels, Samael, Zakun.*

Lahatiel (Lahtiel): Lahatiel is, according to an ancient Jewish legend, overseer of the gates of death leading into Hell. He is said to be leader of an order of angels called the Lehatim. He is an angel of punishment in Hell.

See *punishment (angels of).*

Lailah (Leliel or Laylah): Lailah is the Jewish Angel of Night. Whenever a woman conceives, Lailah takes the sperm to God, who then decides what sort of person the resulting child will become. After this, God orders a soul to enter the embryo, and an angel stands guard to prevent it from escaping. Lailah looks after all matters relating to conception and pregnancy.

Lailiel: According to the Third Book of Enoch, Lailiel is one of the Rulers of the Earth and is responsible for the night.

See *Rulers of the Earth.*

Lauviah (La-vee-yah) **(Lauiah, Laviah, or Luviah):** Lauviah has been called both a Throne and a Cherubim. Others say he is a fallen angel. Lauviah is one of the seventy-two Schemhamphoras, a group of angels who bear the various names of God found in Jewish scriptures. He is guardian angel of people born between May 11 and 16 and between June 11 and 15. Lauviah promotes positive thought and is considered an angel of joy and happiness.

See *Cherubim, fallen angels, guardian angels, Schemhamphoras, Thrones.*

Lecabel (Lay-ka-bel): Lecabel looks after plant life and is especially interested in agriculture. Lecabel is one of the seventy-two Schemhamphoras, a group of angels who bear the various names of God found in Jewish scriptures. He is also guardian angel of people born between August 23 and 28. Lecabel helps people develop their skills and talents.

See *guardian angels, Schemhamphoras*.

Lehahiah (Lay-ha-hee-yah): Lehahiah belongs to the Schemhamphoras, a group of seventy-two angels who bear the various names of God found in Jewish scriptures. He is guardian angel of people born between September 8 and 12.

See *guardian angels, Schemhamphoras*.

Lelahel (Lay-lar-hel): Lelahel is one of the eight Seraphim named in the Kabbalah. He is one of the seventy-two Schemhamphoras, a group of angels who bear the various names of God found in Jewish scriptures, and guardian angel of people born between April 15 and 20. Lelahel can be called upon for good health and success in worthwhile activities.

See *guardian angels, Schemhamphoras, Seraphim*.

Leviah (Loo-vee-yah) **(Leuviah or Leuuiah):** Leviah is one of the seventy-two Schemhamphoras, a group of angels who bear the various names of God found in Jewish scriptures. He is guardian angel of people born between June 22 and 26. He helps people set goals and work hard until they achieve them.

See *guardian angels, Schemhamphoras*.

Leviathan: In the First Book of Enoch, Leviathan is referred to as a demon and is the female equivalent to Satan. Medieval writers sometimes considered Leviathan to be king of the fallen angels. In the Jewish tradition, Leviathan is an angel of death.

See *death (angel of), demon, fallen angels, Satan*.

Liberating Angel: The Shekinah is called the liberating angel in the Kabbalah.

See *Shekinah*.

Lilith: In the Jewish tradition, Lilith is a female demon who preys on babies and young children. According to this tradition, she was married to Adam before Eve, and produced one hundred children every day, Cain among them. She was furious when Eve was created and has worked against humankind ever since. She is reputed to now be married to Samael.

See *demon*, *Samael*.

Liwel (Liwet): Liwel is an angel of creativity who can be called upon when you have doubts about your creative abilities. Liwel also helps lovers develop their relationships.

Lord, Angel of the: The Angel of the Lord appeared many times in the Bible. There is some confusion as to whether or not this term refers to the same angel each time, or even if "Angel of the Lord" denotes God himself. The Angel of the Lord appeared to Hagar, a servant girl, on two occasions. It is generally believed that the Angel of the Lord who appeared to Moses in the burning bush was Archangel Michael. Some authorities believe Archangel Uriel is the Angel of the Lord. An Angel of the Lord appeared to Zacharias to tell him that he and his wife would give birth to John the Baptist. During the course of the conversation, this angel identified himself as Archangel Gabriel (Luke 1:11–20).

See *Archangels*, *Gabriel*, *Hagar*, *Michael*.

Love, Angel of: See *Shekinah*.

Lucifer: Lucifer is one of the most important fallen angels. Originally, Lucifer, which means "bringer of light," referred to the planet Venus. The name "Lucifer" became attached to Satan by mistake. The Bible tells how King Nebuchadnezzar thought he'd promote himself to the level of God. Isaiah attacked the king when he wrote: "How art thou fallen from Heaven, O Lucifer, son of the morning!" (Isaiah 14:12). "Son of the morning" refers to Venus as the morning star, which is brighter than all the other heavenly bodies, except for the sun and moon. Two early Christian theologians, Tertullian and St. Augustine, connected Satan with the morning star because of this reference in Isaiah, and Satan has been called Lucifer ever since.

Satan was originally one of the mighty Archangels and governed Heaven. However, pride was his downfall. One charming medieval story says that Lucifer had a seat next to the throne of God. One day, when God left his seat, Lucifer promptly sat in it, which horrified Archangel Michael so much that he fought Lucifer and cast him out of Heaven.

See *Archangels, fallen angels, Michael, Satan.*

Lumiel: In the Kabbalah, Lumiel is sometimes considered to be the angel of the earth. He is sometimes considered to be both a planetary angel and an Archangel. However, Sandalphon and Uriel are more usually associated with the element of earth. Lumiel has always been controversial, and many people consider him a "dark angel."

See *Archangels, dark angels, planetary angels, Sandalphon, Uriel.*

Machidiel (Malahidael): Machidiel is one of the angels of the Tree of Life, and he is frequently invoked by people performing love magic. Machidiel is the angel of March, and he looks after the interests of people born under the zodiac sign of Aries. His main task is to help people who lack the necessary courage to express their love to others.

> See *zodiac (angels of the)*.

Madimi: Madimi is one of the Enochian angels who communicated with Dr. John Dee and Edward Kelley in the sixteenth century. Madimi appeared as a young, golden-haired girl wearing a green-and-red dress.

> See *Dee (Dr. John)*, *Enochian angels*.

Madimiel: In the Jewish Kabbalah, Madimiel is the angel responsible for the planet Mars.

Mahasiah (Mar-hah-see-yah): Mahasiah is one of the seventy-two Schemhamphoras, a group of angels who bear the various names of God found in Jewish scriptures. Mahasiah is also guardian angel for people born between April 10 and 14. He is a cheerful angel who helps people maintain a positive disposition.

See *guardian angels, Schemhamphoras*.

Maion: Maion is ruler of the planet Saturn and he helps people who are prepared to work hard to achieve their goals. Maion is the angel to invoke whenever you need self-control or self-discipline.

Malahidael: Malahidael can be invoked whenever you need the necessary courage to stand up for what you believe is right. It is highly likely that Malahidael and Machidiel are the same angel.

See *Machidiel*.

Malaika (Malaka): In Islam, malaika are angels who look after mankind. They also record mankind's good and bad deeds. There are various ranks of malaika. The *al-mukarrubun* are the malaika angels closest to Allah. Their task is to worship and praise him twenty-four hours a day. At the other extreme is *malak al mawt*, the keeper of Hell, who is an angel of death. *Malak al mawt* is assisted by nineteen helpers called *al-zabaniyya*.

See *death (angel of)*.

Malak Ha-Mavet: In both Jewish and Islamic lore, Malak ha-Mavet is considered an angel of death. He is sometimes thought to be Azrael or Sammael.

See *Azrael, death (angel of), Sammael*.

Malakhim (Malakim): The Malakhim are one of the ten choirs of angels listed in the *Key of Solomon*. They are similar in rank to the Virtues. Bariel, Gabriel, Michael, Raphael, Tarshish, and Uriel are all princes of the order of Malakhim. The Malakhim are considered the most important angels in the hierarchy of angels listed in the Zohar (part of the Kabbalah). Moses Maimonides placed them in sixth position in his hierarchy.

See *hierarchy of angels,* individual angels, *Virtues.*

Malashiel (Maltiel): According to the Kabbalah, Malashiel is a Friday angel who lives in the Third Heaven. He is the preceptor angel of Elijah.

See *preceptor angels.*

Malikim (Malik): In the Islamic tradition, Malikim is the angel who guards the gates of Hell.

Malkhidael (Melchidael or Melkejal): Malkhidael is the Archangel of the astrological sign Aries and rules the month of March. Artists usually depict him wearing green-trimmed red robes, holding the astrological symbol of Aries.

See *Archangels.*

Malkiel (Malkhiel or Malquiel): Malkiel is one of the three angelic princes in the Kabbalah. In the Book of Raziel, Malkiel is said to have power over fire and flame. Malkiel provides inspiration, good ideas, and creativity. He promises success to people who are persistent and work hard.

Manadel (Mar-na-del): Manadel is one of the seventy-two Schemhamphoras, a group of angels who bear the various names of God found in Jewish scriptures. He is also guardian angel for people born between February 15 and 19. Manadel looks after people who travel over water and has an interest in animals that live in the sea.

See *guardian angels, Schemhamphoras.*

Manichaeism (Manicheism or Manichaeanism): Manichaeism is a dualistic, Gnostic religion founded by the Persian prophet Mani (c.216–276). At the age of twelve, Mani experienced his first vision of what he called his heavenly twin. This was his guardian angel who protected him and became his spiritual teacher. After a second vision, Mani started preaching in 240 CE, teaching that there were two sources of creation, one good and one evil. God created all the good in the world, while Satan created the evil. The material world was, in effect, an attack on the spiritual world of light by the forces of darkness. The soul of a person was deemed to be light (God), while the physical body was dark (Satan). Mani's religion aimed to release the light that was imprisoned within the darkness. He claimed that he, Buddha, Jesus, and Zoroaster had been sent to help humanity achieve this. Manichaeism grew rapidly. The Zoroastrians were appalled at how popular it became and tried to abolish the religion by imprisoning Mani. When he was put on trial, Mani claimed that he had received his doctrine from God, and it had been taught to him by his angel. Mani's death is shrouded in mystery. He possibly died in prison, or may have been executed or crucified. Manichaeism survived the death of its founder and spread as far as China in the East, and Spain in the West. Traces of it survived until the thirteenth century.

See *guardian angels, Jesus, Satan, Zoroaster, Zoroastrianism.*

Manna: Manna is the food of the angels. God sent manna to the Israelites to sustain them during the forty years they wandered in the wilderness: "Then said the Lord unto Moses, Behold, I will rain bread from Heaven for you; and the people shall go out and gather a certain rate every day, that I may prove them, whether they shall walk in my law, or no" (Exodus 16:4). The Israelites found the manna growing on the arid land they were crossing, and they turned it into bread. They called it "bread from Heaven."

Later, Jesus referred to himself as the "true bread from Heaven": "Verily, verily, I say unto you, Moses gave you not that bread from Heaven; but my Father giveth you the true bread from Heaven. For the bread of God is he which cometh down from Heaven, and giveth life unto the world" (John 6:32–33). Angels are believed to eat manna in Heaven. However, as angels are spiritual beings, there is some doubt as to why they would need food.

Mansions of the Moon: The mansions of the moon represent the twenty-eight days it takes the moon to complete its lunar cycle. Each day of the cycle represents a different mansion. Early astrologers used the mansions to follow the course of the seasons. It is possible that this division of the Heavens is older than the better-known signs of the zodiac. Different versions of the mansions of the moon can be found in Arabic, Babylonian, Chinese, Egyptian, Indian, and Persian astrology. Arabic astrologers were greatly influenced by the twenty-eight mansions—the symbolic importance of the crescent moon in Islam and the twenty-eight letters of the Arabic alphabet, which perfectly matched the twenty-eight-day lunar cycle, made a powerful magical combination. Arabic magicians adopted the mansions of the moon and assigned a variety of associations to each one. This enabled them to construct powerful talismans that were consecrated when the specific mansion was rising in the eastern horizon. Not surprisingly, medieval magicians also created a number of associations for the different mansions of the moons. Magicians today still use the mansions of the moon to ensure their magic is performed at the most propitious time. Here are the twenty-eight mansions, with the angels and virtues described by Cornelius Agrippa in his *Three Books of Occult Philosophy* (1531):

First Mansion
   Name: Alnath (Horns of Aries)
   Angel: Geniel
   Zodiac sign: Aries
   Virtues: "It causeth discords, and journeys."

Second Mansion
   Name: Allothaim or Albochan (Belly of Aries)
   Angel: Enediel
   Zodiac sign: Aries

Virtues: "Conduceth to the finding of treasures, and to the retaining of captives."

Third Mansion

Name: Achaomazon or Athoray (Showering or Pleiades)
Angel: Anixiel
Zodiac sign: Aries
Virtues: "Profitable to sailors, huntsmen, and alchemists."

Fourth Mansion

Name: Aldebaram or Aldelamen (Eye or Head of Taurus)
Angel: Azariel
Zodiac sign: Taurus
Virtues: "Causeth the destruction and hinderances of build-ings, fountains, wells, of gold mines, the flight of creeping things, and begetteth discord."

Fifth Mansion

Name: Alchatay or Albachay
Angel: Gabriel
Zodiac sign: Taurus
Virtues: "Helpeth to the return from a journey, to the instruc-tion of scholars, it confirmeth edifices, it giveth health and good will."

Sixth Mansion

Name: Alhanna or Alchaya (Little Star of Great Light)
Angel: Dirachiel
Zodiac sign: Gemini
Virtues: "Conduceth to hunting, and besieging of towns, and revenge of princes, it destroyeth harvests and fruits and hindereth the operation of the physician."

Seventh Mansion

Name: Aldimiach or Alarzach (Arm of Gemini)
Angel: Scheliel
Zodiac sign: Gemini

Virtues: "It conferreth gain and friendship, it's profitable to lovers, it feareth flies, destroyeth magisteries."

Eighth Mansion

Name: Alnaza or Anatrachya (Misty or Cloudy)

Angel: Amnediel

Zodiac sign: Cancer

Virtues: "It causeth love, friendship, and society of fellow travelers, it driveth away mice and afflicteth captives, confirming their imprisonment."

Ninth Mansion

Name: Archaam or Arcapth (Eye of the Lion)

Angel: Barbiel

Zodiac sign: Cancer-Leo

Virtues: "It hindereth harvests and travelers, and putteth discord between men."

Tenth Mansion

Name: Algelioche or Albgebh (Neck or Forehead of Leo)

Angel: Ardifiel

Zodiac sign: Leo

Virtues: "It strengtheneth buildings, yieldeth love, benevolence and help against enemies."

Eleventh Mansion

Name: Azobra or Arduf (Hair of the Lion's Head)

Angel: Neciel

Zodiac sign: Leo

Virtues: "It is good for voyages, and gain by merchandise, and for redemption of captives."

Twelfth Mansion

Name: Alzarpha or Azarpha (Tail of Leo)

Angel: Abdizuel

Zodiac sign: Leo

Virtues: "It giveth prosperity to harvests, and plantations, but hindereth seamen, but it is good for the bettering of servants, captives and companions."

Thirteenth Mansion

Name: Alhaire (Dog Stars or the Wings of Virgo)
Angel: Jazeriel
Zodiac sign: Virgo
Virtues: "It is prevalent for benevolence, gain, voyages, harvests, and freedom of captives."

Fourteenth Mansion

Name: Achureth or Arimet, or possibly, Azimeth or Alhumech or Alcheymech (Spike of Virgo or Flying Spike)
Angel: Ergediel
Zodiac sign: Virgo
Virtues: "It causeth the love of married folk, it cureth the sick, it's profitable to sailors, but it hindereth journeys by land."

Fifteenth Mansion

Name: Agrapha or Algarpha (Covered or Covered Flying)
Angel: Ataliel
Zodiac sign: Libra
Virtues: "It's profitable for the extracting of treasures, for digging of pits, it helpeth forward divorce, discord, and the destruction of houses and enemies, and hindereth travelers."

Sixteenth Mansion

Name: Azubene or Ahubene (Horns of Scorpio)
Angel: Azeruel
Zodiac sign: Scorpio
Virtues: "It hindereth journeys and wedlock, harvests and merchandise, it prevaileth for redemption of captives."

Seventeenth Mansion

Name: Alchil (Crown of Scorpio)
Angel: Adriel

Zodiac sign: Scorpio

Virtues: "It bettereth a bad fortune, maketh love durable, strengtheneth buildings, and helpeth seamen."

Eighteenth Mansion

Name: Alchas or Altob (Heart of Scorpio)

Angel: Egibiel

Zodiac sign: Scorpio

Virtues: "It causeth discord, sedition, conspiracy against princes and mighty ones, and revenge from enemies, but it freeth captives and helpeth edifices."

Nineteenth Mansion

Name: Allatha or Achala, or possibly Hycula or Axala (Tail of Scorpio)

Angel: Amutiel

Zodiac sign: Scorpio

Virtues: "It helpeth in the besieging of cities and taking of towns, and in the driving of men from their places, and for the destruction of seamen, and perdition of captives."

Twentieth Mansion

Name: Abnahaya (a Beam)

Angel: Kyriel

Zodiac sign: Sagittarius

Virtues: "It helpeth for the taming of wild beasts, for the strengthening of prisons, it destroyeth the wealth of societies, it compelleth a man to come to a certain place."

Twenty-first Mansion

Name: Abeda or Albedach (a Defeat)

Angel: Bethnael

Zodiac sign: Capricorn

Virtues: "It is good for harvests, gain, buildings and travelers, and causeth divorce."

Twenty-second Mansion

Name: Sadahacha, Zodeboluch, or Zandeldena (a Pastor)
Angel: Geliel
Zodiac sign: Capricorn
Virtues: "It promoteth the flight of servants and captives, that they may escape, and helpeth in the curing of diseases."

Twenty-third Mansion

Name: Zabadola or Zobrach (Swallowing)
Angel: Requiel
Zodiac sign: Capricorn
Virtues: "It maketh for divorce, liberty of captives and the health of the sick."

Twenty-fourth Mansion

Name: Sadabath or Chadezoad (Star of Fortune)
Angel: Abrinael
Zodiac sign: Aquarius
Virtues: "It is prevalent for the benevolence of married folk, for the victory of soldiers, it hurteth the execution of government, and hindereth that it may not be exercised."

Twenty-fifth Mansion

Name: Sadalabra or Sadalachia (a Butterfly or a Spreading Forth)
Angel: Aziel
Zodiac sign: Aquarius
Virtues: "It helpeth besieging and revenge, it destroyeth enemies, maketh divorce, confirmeth prisons and buildings, hasteneth messengers, it conduceth to spells against copulation, and so bindeth every member of man, that it cannot perform his duty."

Twenty-sixth Mansion

Name: Alpharg or Phragol Mocaden (the First Drawing)
Angel: Tagriel
Zodiac sign: Aquarius-Pisces

Virtues: "It maketh for the union and love of men, for the health of captives, it destroyeth prisons and buildings."

Twenty-seventh Mansion
Name: Alcharya or Alhalgalmoad (the Second Drawing)
Angel: Atheniel
Zodiac sign: Pisces
Virtues: "It increaseth harvests, revenues, gain, it healeth infirmities, but hindereth buildings, prolongeth prisons, causeth danger to seamen, and helpeth to infer mischiefs on whom you shall please."

Twenty-eighth Mansion
Name: Albotham or Alchalcy (Pisces)
Angel: Amnixiel
Zodiac sign: Pisces
Virtues: "It increaseth harvests and merchandise, it secureth travelers through dangerous places, it maketh for the joy of married couples, but it strengtheneth prisons, and causeth loss of treasures."

See individual angels.

Maonghah (Moun-g-hah): Maonghah is the yazata angel in Zoroastrianism who rules over the moon. Hvare-Khshaeta rules over the sun.

See *Hvare-Khshaeta, yazata, Zoroastrianism.*

Mariokh: Mariokh and Ariukh are the two angels who watched over the family of Enoch (later to become Metatron) to protect and preserve them from the impending Flood. Their actions saved Enoch's bloodline and preserved his writings.

See *Ariukh, Metatron.*

Martin of Cochem: Martin of Cochem (1630–1712) was a German priest who wrote many books, including *Das grosse Leben Christi*, which explained what Heaven was like. Martin saw it as a physical, rather than spiritual, place. Consequently, his Heaven contained rivers, trees, fruits, and flowers. At Easter time in Martin's Heaven, the angels performed plays to entertain the saints and other people in Heaven. The celebrations lasted for fifty days, and the entertainments often lasted all night. The angels proved to be good actors and performed parables, pageants, comedies, and dramas, usually concerning the life and passion of Christ. One of the highlights was the choir of Archangels who enjoyed the opportunity to pay homage to Christ.

See *Archangels*.

Marut: Marut and Harut are two Islamic angels who came down from Heaven to teach humans how to govern themselves. Unfortunately, they revealed the secret name of God to a human woman who used this power to visit the planet Venus. The two angels were punished for their transgressions, and they are imprisoned, head downwards, in a pit near Babylon. They are considered fallen angels.

See *fallen angels, Harut*.

Mashit (Mashitt or Mashhit): In Judaism, Mashit is considered the angel of death for children. In the Zohar, Mashit is one of three demons in Hell who punish people who commit idolatry, incest, and murder. The other two demons are Af and Hemah.

See *Af, death (angel of), Hemah*.

Masleh: According to Jewish tradition, Masleh is the angel in charge of the zodiac. His name possibly comes from *mazloth*, the Hebrew word for "zodiac."

See *zodiac (angels of the)*.

Masniel: Masniel is one of the ruling angels of the zodiac and is responsible for the sign of Libra.

See *zodiac (angels of the)*.

Mastema: Mastema is a fallen angel. He tried to kill Moses to prevent him from asking Pharaoh to set his people free. He also taught the Egyptian magicians feats of conjuring, such as turning a rod into a snake, to undermine the feats of Moses. In the Book of Jubilees, it was Mastema, not God, who tempted Abraham to sacrifice his son Isaac. Mastema, the accusing angel, is often said to be Satan.

See *fallen angels, Satan.*

Matariel (Matarel or Matriel): According to the Third Book of Enoch, Matariel is one of the Rulers of the Earth and is responsible for rain.

See *Rulers of the Earth.*

Mebahel (May-ba-hel): Mebahel is one of the seventy-two Schemhamphoras, a group of angels who bear the various names of God found in Jewish scriptures. Mebahel is also guardian angel to people born between May 26 and May 31. Mebahel encourages friendship and conversation.

See *guardian angels, Schemhamphoras.*

Mebahiah (Me-ba-hee-yah): Mebahiah is one of the seventy-two Schemhamphoras, a group of angels who bear the various names of God found in Jewish scriptures. He is also guardian angel of people born between December 22 and 26. He has a strong interest in philosophy and ethics.

See *guardian angels, Schemhamphoras.*

Mediator Angels: Mediator angels listen to people's prayers and deliver them to God. Guardian angels are good examples of mediator angels. In Judaism, Islam, Christianity, and Zoroastrianism, Archangels act as mediators between God and individual countries. Michael, for instance, mediates between God and Israel. In Zoroastrianism, the Amesha Spentas mediate between God and the people of Persia.

See *Amesha Spentas, Archangels, guardian angels, Islam, Michael, Zoroastrianism*.

Meher: Meher is the yazata angel of light, mercy, and justice. He comforts the soul as it journeys into the underworld.

See *yazata, Zoroastrianism*.

Mehiel (May-hee-el)**:** According to Jewish mysticism, Mehiel looks after writers, scholars, teachers, and communicators. Mehiel is also guardian angel to people born between February 5 and 9. It is possible that Mehiel and Mehikiel are the same angel.

See *guardian angels, Mehikiel*.

Mehikiel: Mehikiel is one of the seventy-two Schemhamphoras, a group of angels who bear the various names of God found in Jewish scriptures. It is possible that Mehiel and Mehikiel are the same angel.

See *Mehiel, Schemhamphoras*.

Melahel (May-la-hel)**:** Melahel is one of the seventy-two Schemhamphoras, a group of angels who bear the various names of God found in Jewish scriptures. Melahel, a nurturing and protective angel, is also guardian angel of people born between July 12 and 16.

See *guardian angels, Schemhamphoras*.

Melchizedek (Melchisedek): Melchizedek belongs to the order of Virtues. He is an Angel of the Presence, and one of the most powerful angels in Heaven. Dionysius the Areopagite wrote that he was the angel most loved and favored by God. St. Hippolytus (170–235), the Christian leader and antipope, considered Melchizedek to be more important than Jesus Christ. This may be because, in a papyrus fragment found in Qumran, Melchizedek is said to be a saviour who will bring peace to earth in the final days (11Q Melch). In the Book of Mormon, Melchizedek is the prince of peace. According to Jewish legend, Melchizedek delivered God's covenant to Abraham and prepared the way for the coming of Jesus. One legend says that he spent a hundred years on earth four thousand years ago and established a school to teach people about God. He performs a similar task in Heaven today. Consequently, Melchizedek is normally depicted as a teacher or lecturer, holding a scroll in one hand with the other hand raised as if to emphasize what he is saying. Melchizedek can be called upon whenever you need peace, tranquility, and the love of God.

See *Dionysius the Areopagite, Presence (Angels of the), Virtues.*

Melek Ta'us (Malak Ta'us): Melek Ta'us is known as the Peacock Angel and is the main Archangel in the belief system of the Yazidis.

See *Archangels, Yazidi.*

Memunnim: "Appointed Ones." The memunnim are a choir of angels mentioned in the Third Book of Enoch. During the Middle Ages, they became associated with guardian angels and are involved with every event, large or small, that takes place anywhere in the world.

See *guardian angels.*

Menadel (Mehn-ah-del)**:** Menadel is one of the seventy-two Schemhamphora angels. He is guardian angel to people born between September 18 and 23. He ensures that people living away from their home lands keep the memory and love of their native country in their hearts.

See *guardian angels, Schemhamphoras.*

Meniel: Meniel is one of the seventy-two Schemhamphoras, a group of angels who bear the various names of God found in Jewish scriptures.

See *Schemhamphoras.*

Mephistopheles: Mephistopheles was originally an Archangel. He then became a fallen angel and is now one of the seven great princes in Hell. He was involved in the war in Heaven and became a fallen angel. Today he is one of the seven great princes in Hell.

See *Archangels, fallen angels.*

Merkabah: In Jewish mysticism, the Merkabah is the divine char-iot that is supported by angels called Hayyoth. There is a whole branch of religious writing based on this chariot, which began with the vision of Ezekiel (Ezekiel 1). According to the Talmud, Sandalphon stands behind the chariot. The Merkabah is also a form of Jewish mysticism that flourished for a thousand years until it was succeeded by the Kabbalah. In the Merkabah, the names of angels and the secret names of God were used to ascend through the various Heavens until the throne-chariot of God was reached.

See *Hayyoth, Sandalphon.*

Metatron: Metatron is Chancellor of Heaven, a member of the Sarim, and one of the leaders of the Seraphim. Metatron is the most important angel in Jewish lore, which probably accounts for his name, which means "the throne beside the throne of God." He is sometimes known as the "Lesser YHWH," YHWH being the four letters of the unspeakable name of God. In the Third Book of Enoch, Metatron is said to sit on a throne where he dispenses jus-tice. According to legend, Metatron was originally Enoch, Adam's great-great-great-great-grandson, who lived for 365 years on earth before "God took him" and turned him into an angel (Genesis 5:23–24). Metatron, the angel, is almost as large as the world. He has 36 pairs of wings and 365,000 eyes, each of them as bright as the sun. Enoch had been a scribe before his transformation and has con-tinued working as God's secretary and archivist. Metatron sits on a beautiful throne at the entrance to the Seventh Heaven. Because he has lived as a human, Metatron is frequently called the Angel of Mankind. In Jewish belief, Metatron carries Jewish prayers through 900 Heavens directly to God. According to the Zohar, Metatron combines both human and angelic perfection, and this serves him in good stead in his role of ruling the entire world. Fortunately, he has seventy angelic princes to help him in this work. You should call on Metatron whenever you are engaged in deep thought.

See *Sarim, Seraphim.*

Micah: Micah is dedicated to the spiritual growth of mankind. You can invoke Micah if you are pursuing a spiritual path.

Michael (Mi-ka-el)**:** "Who is like God." The Archangel Michael is the greatest angel in Christianity, Islam, and Judaism. This is not surprising, as Michael is God's most important warrior angel, and he fights for everything that is good, honorable, and righteous. Michael is Ruler of the Order of Virtues, Chief of the Archangels, Archangel of the Sun (Michael Shemeshel), Prince of the Presence, Prince of the Sarim, Prince of the Seraphim, and Angel of Repentance. He is also one of the seventy-two Schemhamphoras. Michael and Gabriel are the only two angels mentioned by name in the Bible. (Raphael appears in the Book of Tobit.) In Daniel 10:13, he is described as "Michael, one of the chief princes," and in Daniel 12:1 he is "the great prince which standeth for the children of thy people." Michael threw Satan out of Heaven after the battle between the good and evil angels (Revelation 12:7–9). According to the Book of Adam and Eve, Michael helped Adam after his expulsion from the Garden of Eden. He taught him how to farm and later gave him a tour of Heaven. After his death, Michael persuaded God to allow his soul to enter Heaven. According to Jewish legend, Michael prevented Abraham from sacrificing his son Isaac. He was also the angel who appeared to Moses in a burning bush. He freed Peter from prison and rescued Daniel from the lion's den. Michael also has the task of accompanying souls back to Heaven after physical death. Michael is often shown wearing armour or chain mail, wielding a large sword. His wings are emerald green. He often has one foot resting on a serpent or dragon, symbolizing his defeat of the devil. Michael is also often depicted carrying scales, as he has the important task of weighing souls to determine their worthiness at the Last Judgment.

In Islam, Michael is known as Mikhail.

See *Archangels, Gabriel, Mikhail, Raphael, Sarim, Satan, Schemhamphoras, Seraphim, Virtues.*

Mihael (Mi-ha-el): According to the Kabbalah, Mihael is the angel of fertility and fidelity. He belongs to the choir of Virtues and is guardian angel to people born between November 18 and 22. Mihael can be invoked for happiness and to ensure loyalty and faithfulness.

See *guardian angels, Virtues.*

Mihr: Mihr is the angel of business relationships. Mihr can be called upon to help develop these relationships further, and if desired, turn them into friendships.

Mikael (Mik-ah-el): Mikael may be another form of Michael. He is guardian angel of people born between October 19 and 23. He is an angel of prosperity and well-being.

See *guardian angels, Michael.*

Mikhail (Mika'il or Mikal): Mikhail is one of the four Archangels in Islam. He is described as having wings of emerald-green and hair of saffron. Each strand of hair has a million faces with a million mouths and a million tongues. Using all of his mouths, Mikhail pleads with Allah to forgive all the sins of mankind. The Cherubim were created from Mikhail's tears. Mikhail is the Islamic equivalent of Michael.

See *Archangels, Cherubim, Michael.*

Miniel: Miniel was a popular angel in medieval times, as people believed he could be invoked to induce passion in even the most reluctant woman. For best results, you had to face south when invoking Miniel.

Ministering Angels: The ministering angels live in the Seventh Heaven and cater to God's immediate needs. They are the only angels in the Seventh Heaven that can be seen by human eyes. According to Jewish legend, ministering angels attended to the needs of Adam and Eve while they were living in the Garden of Eden. Ministering angels, apparently under the direction of Archangel Michael, gave advice to Noah and his descendants. Guardian angels are also sometimes called ministering angels because they attend to their charges.

See *Archangels, guardian angels, Michael.*

Mithra: Mithra is the angel of light in Zoroastrianism. Mithra is a yazata angel who mediates between mankind and God and also helps Rashnu and Sraosha judge the souls of people when they die. Mithra is said to have ten thousand eyes. Mithra is a leading member of the Izad, the twenty-eight important angels that constantly surround Ahura Mazda. Mithra's birthday is said to be December 25.

See *Ahura Mazda, Izad, Rashnu, Sraosha, yazata, Zoroastrianism.*

Mizrael (Mits-rah-el) **(Mitzrael or Mitrael):** In the Kabbalah, Mizrael is considered an Archangel. He is also one of the seventy-two Schemhamphoras, a group of angels who bear the various names of God found in Jewish scriptures. Mizrael is guardian angel of people born between January 16 and 20. He helps creative and talented people develop their skills.

See *Archangels, guardian angels, Schemhamphoras.*

Mons, Angels of: In August 1914, during World War I, a battle took place between a strong German force and an outnumbered British, French, and Belgian force near the town of Mons, Belgium. A number of apparitions were seen by troops from both sides. While the Allied forces were struggling to retreat, both sides suddenly stopped shooting and gazed awestruck at four or five huge white-robed angels. Other apparitions were also seen at this time. On August 28, a number of British soldiers saw three-winged and robed figures in the sky above the German lines. They remained visible for forty-five minutes.

Unfortunately, these momentous events became confused when one month later, a story called "The Bowmen" by Arthur Machen was published in the *Evening News*. This story tells how British soldiers were saved by the appearance of the spirits of English bowmen who had fought in the Battle of Agincourt in 1415. As his story was published at the same time as people were talking about the occurrences in Belgium, Machen's bowmen became known as the "angels of Mons."

Monthly Angels: These are angels that govern each month of the year.

> January: Gabriel
> February: Barchiel
> March: Machidiel
> April: Asmodel
> May: Ambriel
> June: Muriel
> July: Verchiel
> August: Hamaliel
> September: Uriel
> October: Barbiel
> November: Adnachiel
> December: Hanael

> See individual angels.

Moon Angels: At least partly thanks to Henry Wadsworth Longfellow (1807–1882) and his poem, "The Golden Legend," Archangel Gabriel is usually considered "the angel of the moon, who brings the gift of hope to mankind." However, in later versions of this poem, Longfellow changed the name to Onafiel. As there is no angel of that name, it appears that Longfellow accidentally misspelled Ofaniel (Ophaniel). There are many other possible claimants to the moniker of moon angel, including Abuzohar, Elimiel, Iachadiel, Tsaphiel, Yahriel, and Zachariel.

The moon plays an important role in magic, and it is divided into twenty-eight mansions, known as mansions of the moon, which symbolize each day of the lunar month. Each mansion has its own guardian angel, and Cornelius Agrippa listed these almost five hundred years ago: 1. Geniel; 2. Enediel; 3. Anixiel; 4. Azariel; 5. Gabriel; 6. Dirachiel; 7. Scheliel; 8. Amnediel; 9. Barbiel; 10. Ardifiel; 11. Neciel; 12. Abdizuel; 13. Jazeriel; 14. Ergediel; 15. Ataliel; 16. Azeruel; 17. Adriel; 18. Egibiel; 19. Amutiel; 20. Kyriel; 21. Bethnael; 22. Geliel; 23. Requiel; 24. Abrinael; 25. Aziel; 26. Tagriel; 27. Atheniel; 28. Amnixiel. (Henry Cornelius Agrippa, *Three Books of Occult Philosophy*, Llewellyn Publications, 1993, page 533.)

See *Archangels, Gabriel, guardian angels*, individual angels, *mansions of the moon*.

Moroni: Moroni is the angel who appeared to Joseph Smith, founder of the Church of Latter Day Saints, in 1823. Four years later, in 1827, Moroni told him where to dig up the golden plates that contained the Book of Mormon. This was at Hill Cumorah, four miles south of Palmyra, New York. The text was engraved on the plates in hieroglyphics, which Joseph Smith was able to translate. Today, a forty-foot statue of Moroni stands on the site to commemorate this discovery. According to the Book of Mormon, Moroni was the son of Mormon, and the last leader of the Nephites. When Moroni died, he was transformed into an angel.

Mumijah (Moo-mee-yah) **(Mumiah):** Mumijah is one of the seventy-two Schemhamphoras, a group of angels who bear the various names of God found in Jewish scriptures. Mumijah is the guardian angel of people born between March 16 and 20. He provides motivation to people who ask for it.

See *guardian angels, Schemhamphoras*.

Munkar: Munkar and Nakir are Islamic angels of mercy. They are black angels with penetrating blue eyes and long, fine hair. They wear robes of blue light. Their task is to question recently deceased people in their graves about their faith. They also examine the souls to see if they are worthy enough to be allowed into paradise.
See *Islam, Nakir*.

Muriel: Muriel is one of the four regents of the choir of Dominions. He is considered the Archangel responsible for the sign of Cancer, and he also looks after the month of July. Muriel can be invoked whenever your emotions need to be kept under control.
See *Archangels, Dominions, zodiac (angels of the)*.

Murmur: Murmur is a fallen angel who is now a duke in Hell with thirty legions of demons at his command. He spends most of his time teaching philosophy. Before his fall, he belonged to both the order of Thrones and the order of Angels.
See *Angels, demon, fallen angels, Thrones*.

Nabo (Nabu or Nebo): Nabo was originally a sukallin angel. Today, Nabo is one of the angels in Heaven who record the good and bad deeds of humankind. At one time the Babylonians and Chaldeans considered him a god. He later became messenger for the god Marduk and ultimately became a recording angel.

See *Sukallin.*

Nairyosangha (Ny-ry-o-sarng-ha): Nairyosangha is a yazata angel in Zoroastrianism who serves as a messenger for Ahura Mazda. Nairyosangha also carries prayers to Heaven.

See *Ahura Mazda, yazata, Zoroastrianism.*

Nakhiel (Nachiel): Nakhiel is the angel of the sun who helps Archangel Michael look after the sun.

See *Archangels, Michael.*

Nakir: Nakir and Munkar are Islamic angels of mercy. They are black angels with blue eyes. Their task is to question people in their graves about their faith.

See *Islam (angels of), Munkar.*

Nalvage: On April 10, 1584, an Enochian angel called Nalvage began communicating with Dr. John Dee and his scryer, Edward Kelley. He dictated a tablet that Dee could use to work out the duties of different angels in the Enochian hierarchy.

See *Dee (Dr. John)*, *Enochian angels*.

Nanael (Nar-nah-el): Nanael belongs to the choir of Principalities and is one of the seventy-two Schemhamphoras. He is the guardian angel of people born between December 13 and 16. Nanael helps people involved in law and order.

See *guardian angels*, *Principalities*, *Schemhamphoras*.

Nathanael: Nathanael is a prince of the Seraphim. Despite the slight difference in spelling, it is likely that he is Nathanel.

See *Nathanel*, *Seraphim*.

Nathanel (Nathaniel, Nataniel, or Xathanael): According to Jewish legend, Nathanel is one of the angels of fire. In this role he rescued seven men whom the pagan King Jair had sentenced to death by burning. After rescuing the men from the raging fire, Nathanel gave the king and his servants the punishment that had been meted out to the seven men. Nathanel also reputedly taught King Solomon when he was a young man.

See *Xathanael*.

Neciel: Neciel is one of the twenty-eight angels who govern the mansions of the moon. Neciel is responsible for Azobra, the eleventh mansion. Neciel helps travelers and people engaged in business. He also helps the redemption of prisoners.

See *mansions of the moon*.

Nelakhel (Nel-a-kel) (Nelchael): Nelakhel is something of a mystery. Some authorities say he is a member of the choir of Thrones, and one of the seventy-two Schemhamphoras, a group of angels who bear the various names of God found in Jewish scriptures.

Others say he is a fallen angel. However, he is guardian angel of people born between July 2 and 6. In this role, he helps people develop a sense of responsibility for their actions.

See *fallen angels, guardian angels, Schemhamphoras, Thrones.*

Nemamiah (Ne-ma-mee-yah): Nemamiah belongs to the choir of Archangels and has a strong interest in just causes. He is particularly interested in the well-being of children and animals. He is one of the seventy-two Schemhamphoras, a group of angels who bear the various names of God found in Jewish scriptures. He is also guardian angel to people born between January 1 and 5. You should invoke Nemamiah whenever you are seeking justice.

See *Archangels, guardian angels, Schemhamphoras.*

Nephilim (Nephillim or Nefilim): The Nephilim were the children born after the Grigori mated with human women. They were argumentative, fierce, ravenous giants who fought against each other and humans. When people refused to give them food, they began eating humans. Jewish legend says it was the Nephilim who built the Tower of Babel. The last of the Nephilim (there were 409,000 of them) died in the Great Flood, and it's possible the flood was created with this aim in mind.

See *Grigori, Shemhazai.*

Nilaihah: Nilaihah is an angel belonging to the choir of Dominions. He is regarded as something of a poet, as he prophesies in rhyme. He helps people who enjoy peace and quiet. Nilaihah is also an angel of harmony and beauty, and he can help people find love and happiness, especially after a setback or disappointment. According to the Kabbalah, Nilaihah can be invoked by reciting any of the divine names of God, followed by the first verse of Psalm 9.

See *Dominions.*

Nithael (Nit-ha-el): Nithael is considered one of the seventy-two Schemhamphoras, a group of angels who bear the various names of God found in Jewish scriptures. However, some authorities consider him a fallen angel. He is guardian angel of people born between December 17 and 21. Nithael encourages people to achieve success in all areas of life.

See *fallen angels, guardian angels, Schemhamphoras.*

Nithhaja (Nit-ha-yah) **(Nilaihah, Nith-Haiah, or Nithaiah):** Nithhaja is a member of the choir of Dominions, and is one of the seventy-two Schemhamphoras, a group of angels who bear the various names of God found in Jewish scriptures. He is interested in hidden mysteries and often speaks in rhyme. He is guardian angel of people born between July 23 and 27. Nithhaja encourages love, happiness, and friendship.

See *Dominions, guardian angels, Schemhamphoras.*

Nogahel (Nogael or Noghael): In the Jewish Kabbalah, Nogahel is the angel responsible for the planet Venus.

Nuriel: Nuriel is sometimes called the angel of fire and hail. The name "Nuriel" comes from *nura,* the Aramaic word for "fire." Nuriel is approximately three and a half miles tall and lives in the Second Heaven. Archangels Gabriel and Michael have also been called angels of fire. In Jewish lore, Nuriel is a strong force against evil.

See *Archangels, Gabriel, Michael.*

Och: Och is one of the seven Olympian spirits who rule over the 196 divisions of Heaven. Och is responsible for 28 of these. He has 35,536 legions of angels to help him in this work. According to some accounts, Och is also responsible for the sun. Och is considered the angel of alchemy, and he is willing to help anyone with a desire for knowledge. Och governed the world from 920 to 1410 CE.

See *Olympian spirits*.

Ofaniel: See *Ophaniel*.

Olympian Spirits: The Olympian spirits are seven angels who rule the 196 divisions of Heaven. They each take turns governing the world for 490 years. Because they relate to the various planets, they are sometimes associated with the planetary angels. Their names are:

Aratron, ruler of 49 provinces. His planet is Saturn.
Bethor, ruler of 42 provinces. His planet is Jupiter.

Hagith, ruler of 21 provinces. His planet is Venus.

Och, ruler of 28 provinces. His planet is the Sun.

Ophiel, ruler of 14 provinces. His planet is Mercury.

Phaleg, ruler of 35 provinces. His planet is Mars.

Phul, ruler of 7 provinces. His planet is the Moon.

The Olympian spirits first appeared in an influential six-teenth-century grimoire called *Arbatel of Magick* (1575), and they have been invoked by magicians ever since.

See individual angels, *planetary angels.*

Omael (Oh-ma-el): Omael belongs to the choir of Dominions, and he is one of the seventy-two Schemhamphoras, a group of angels who bear the various names of God found in Jewish scriptures. He is the guardian angel of people born between August 18 and 22. Some authorities say he is a fallen angel. Omael encourages healthy minds, bodies, and spirits.

See *Dominions, fallen angels, guardian angels, Schemhamphoras.*

Omophorus: In Manichaean belief, the angel Omophorus carried the entire world on his shoulders. In the same system, Splen-ditenes supported the Heavens on his back.

See *Splenditenes.*

Onafiel: Onafiel appears in later editions of Henry Wadsworth Longfellow's poem "The Golden Legend," described as the angel who governed the moon. In earlier editions, this task was credited to Gabriel. Onafiel appears nowhere else, though, and Longfel-low probably accidentally transposed two letters to write Onafiel, instead of Ofaniel (Ophaniel).

See *Gabriel, Ophaniel.*

Ongkanon: Ongkanon is willing to help people express their inner-most feelings, especially on matters concerning love.

Ooniemme: Ooniemme can be called upon whenever you feel grateful and whenever you wish to bless someone.

Ophaniel (Ofaniel or Ophanniel): Ophaniel is one of the leaders of the Cherubim. (However, he has also been called chief of the Thrones.) Ophaniel is one of the Rulers of the Earth and is in charge of the phases of the moon. He is said to have 16 faces, 100 pairs of wings, and 8,766 eyes (equal to the number of hours in a year). Ophaniel's eyes are so powerful that not even other angels can bear to look into them. According to the Third Book of Enoch, it would take a man 2,500 years to climb from his feet to the top of his head.

See *Cherubim, Rulers of the Earth, Thrones.*

Ophanim: The ophanim are a choir of angels mentioned, along with the Seraphim and Cherubim, in the First Book of Enoch. Ophaniel is chief of the ophanim. The ophanim contain numerous eyes and wings, and they have been described as wheels within wheels. Each member of the ophanim has seventy-two sapphires in his robe and four emeralds in his crown. The light emanating from them is so strong that it illuminates the Seventh Heaven, where God lives. Moses Maimonides ranked them in second position in his hierarchy of angels.

See *Cherubim, hierarchy of angels, Ophaniel, Seraphim.*

Ophiel: Ophiel is one of the seven Olympian spirits who rule over the 196 sections of Heaven. Ophiel is responsible for 14 of these. Ophiel is also responsible for the planet Mercury. According to the Olympian spirit system, Ophiel is the current governor of the world. His reign runs from 1900 to 2390 CE.

See *Olympian spirits.*

Orifiel (Orifel, Orfiel, or Oriphiel): Orifiel was called an Archangel by Pope St. Gregory the Great (540–604 CE). However, he does not figure in any other listing of Archangels. He is usually considered a member of the choir of Thrones. He has been called the angel of Saturn, which would make him a planetary angel. In the *Lemegeton* (*The Lesser Key of Solomon*), he is called one of the seven regents of the world.

See *Archangels, planetary angels, Thrones.*

Oriphiel: Rudolf Steiner considered Oriphiel one of the seven great Archangels.

See *Archangels, Orifiel, Steiner (Rudolf).*

Ormazd: In Zoroastrianism, Ormazd is the twin brother of Ahriman, the prince of darkness and evil. Ormazd is Ahriman's complete opposite and is responsible for everything that is good. He is also known as Ahura Mazda.

See *Ahriman, Ahura Mazda, Zoroastrianism.*

Pahaliah (Pa-ha-lee-yah)**:** Pahaliah is one of the seventy-two Schemhamphoras, a group of angels who bear the various names of God found in Jewish scriptures. His special task is to encourage people to accept Christianity. He is also guardian angel of people born between June 27 and July 1. He encourages people to be honest, upright, and fair.

See *guardian angels, Schemhamphoras*.

Pakhiel (Pakiel): Pakhiel is the angel of the astrological sign of Cancer and helps Archangel Muriel look after people born under this sign.

See *Archangels, Muriel*.

Palatinates: The Palatinates are an order of angels. This name is generally considered an alternative name for the choir of Powers in the hierarchy of angels. *The Greater Key of Solomon*, a famous medieval grimoire used by magicians, contains the necessary spells and invocations that apparently summon the Palatinates. A huge amount of preparation and work is required. The main reason anyone would do this is because the Palatinates are believed to be able to make people invisible.

See *hierarchy of angels, Powers*.

Parasim: The parasim are a choir of angels who do nothing but endlessly sing the praises of God. Their leader is Tagas.

See *Tagas*.

Parendi: In Zoroastrianism, Parendi is the female yazata angel of abundance.

See *yazata, Zoroastrianism*.

Paschar: Seven angels, including Paschar, stand in front of the Holy Throne. Paschar's special responsibility is to look after the curtain that surrounds the Seventh Heaven and the Throne of God. This curtain is likely to be a wall of some sort. Paschar has a special interest in divination and enjoys helping people develop their skills at precognition. He can be called upon if you are seeking help in prophecy or divination.

See *Throne of God*.

Passage, Angels of: Angels frequently appear to people who are dying. Shortly before the moment of physical death, many people experience a vision of an angel who gives them comfort, knowing they'll be protected and guided to the other side.

Peace, Angel of: According to the Testament of Benjamin, the angel of peace looks after and guides the souls of good people after they have died. The angel of peace escorted Enoch on his tour of Heaven (recorded in the First Book of Enoch).

In the Roman Catholic Church, Mary the mother of Jesus is often referred to as the Angel of Peace or the Queen of Angels.

See *Queen of Angels*.

Peacock Angel: See *Yazidi*.

Peliel: In Jewish lore, Peliel is considered one of the chiefs of the choir of Virtues. He mentored Jacob, the Old Testament patriarch who is considered father of the people of Israel. It was Jacob who wrestled with a dark angel for an entire night.
See *dark angels, Virtues*.

Penemue: Penemue is one of the leaders of the Grigori, the angels who came down to earth and slept with human women. He taught mankind how to write using ink and paper. He can be invoked to help overcome stupidity.
See *Grigori*.

Peniel: Peniel may have been the angel who wrestled with Jacob for a whole night. However, as the fight occurred at a place called Peniel or Penuel, it is possible that Peniel the angel does not exist. He is believed to live in the Third Heaven. Peniel and Penuel are more than likely the same angel. The Zohar says Samael was the angel who fought Jacob.
See *Peliel, Penuel, Samael*.

Penuel: Penuel is an Archangel and one of the Angels of the Presence. He is also known as the Angel of Repentance. However, as Penuel or Peniel is also the name of the place where Jacob wrestled with an angel, it is likely that Peniel and Penuel are the same angel.
See *Archangels, Peliel, Peniel, Presence (Angels of the)*.

Peri: In the Persian and Arabic traditions, peri are fallen angels. Their leader is Eblis. The peri are said to be beautiful but vengeful spirits. According to Islamic lore, Mohammad tried to convert them.
See *Eblis, fallen angels*.

Perpetiel: Traditionally, there have always been seven Archangels. However, some New Age angelologists have increased the list to twelve. Perpetiel is one of the angels promoted to Archangel rank in this system. Perpetiel can be invoked if you are working on a worthwhile project but are finding it hard to accomplish. Perpetiel will help you achieve success.

See *Archangels*.

Phaleg (Phalec): Phaleg and Adnachiel rule the order of Angels. Phaleg is also considered one of the seven Olympian Spirits who rule over the 196 sections of Heaven. Phaleg is responsible for 35 of these. Phaleg is also responsible for the planet Mars. Phaleg governed the world from 430 to 920 CE.

See *Adnachiel, Olympian spirits*.

Phanuel: See *Raguel*.

Phoenixes: In the Second Book of Enoch, the Phoenixes and Chalkydri are said to be equal in rank to the Seraphim and Cherubim. They have twelve wings and live in either the Fourth or Sixth Heaven. The Phoenixes sang every morning as the sun rose and were famed for the beauty of their voices.

See *Chalkydri, Cherubim, Seraphim*.

Phorlach (Phorlakh or Forlac): Phorlach is the angel of the element earth. He helps Archangel Uriel perform his work.

See *Archangels, Uriel*.

Phul: Phul is one of the seven Olympian Spirits who rule over the 196 sections of Heaven. Phul is responsible for 7 of these. Phul is also responsible for the moon. Phul governed the world from 1040 to 550 BCE, and he will govern again from 2390 to 2880 CE.

See *Olympian spirits*.

Pistis Sophia: A female aeon.

See *aeons, Sophia.*

Planetary Angels: The ancient Romans associated the days of the week with the seven visible planets. This association gradually took on more and more elements, including angels. The first documented evidence of this comes from twelfth-century Spain. Esoteric philosophy flourished at that time, and European scholars began translating valuable books from the past, discovering many insights in the process. Here are the planets and angels that are generally associated with each day of the week:

Sunday: Sun, Michael (also Raphael)
Monday: Moon, Gabriel
Tuesday: Mars, Samael (also Chamuel)
Wednesday: Mercury, Raphael (also Michael)
Thursday: Jupiter, Zadkiel (also Sachiel and Zachariel)
Friday: Venus, Haniel
Saturday: Saturn, Cassiel (also Orifiel and Zaphkiel)

Cornelius Agrippa included a Kabbalistic list of planetary angels in his *Three Books of Occult Philosophy* (page 553):

Saturn: Sabathiel
Jupiter: Zedekiel
Mars: Madimiel
Sun: Semeliel or Semeschia
Venus: Nogahel
Mercury: Cochabiel or Cochabiah
Moon: Jarahel or Levanael

In addition to these angels, there are also Olympian spirits who also look after the planets. These are:

Sun: Och
Moon: Phul
Mars: Phaleg
Mercury: Ophiel

Jupiter: Bethor

Venus: Hagith

Saturn: Aratron

See *day (angels of the)*, individual angels, *Olympian spirits, week (angels of the)*.

Polial (Poi-le-yel) **(Poiel):** Polial is a member of the choir of Principalities and one of the seventy-two Schemhamphoras, a group of angels who bear the various names of God found in Jewish scriptures. He is also guardian angel of people born between December 27 and 31. He encourages people to fully appreciate the richness and privilege of life.

See *guardian angels, Principalities, Schemhamphoras*.

Powers: The Powers are the sixth-highest rank of angels in Dionysius' hierarchy of angels. Enoch believed they were the first angels created by God, but most people believe all the angels were created at the same time. Their task is to ensure that all the laws of the universe work perfectly. Part of this work is to constantly protect all the roads to Heaven. They also make sure humans are protected from the demons who constantly create disharmony in the world. Chamuel is usually considered chief of the choir of Powers. However, Gabriel, Raphael, Verchiel, and even Satan (before he became a fallen angel) have all been considered chief of this choir. Artists usually depict the Powers as large men wearing suits of armour and holding chained demons. They sometimes hold a golden stave in their right hands.

See *demon, fallen angels, hierarchy of angels*, individual angels, *Satan*.

Praise, Angels of: The angels of praise are a group (possibly even a choir) of angels who endlessly sing God's praises. According to Louis Ginzberg's *Legends of the Jews*, the angels of praise were created on the second day of Creation: "The third creations of the second day were the angel hosts, both the ministering angels and the angels of praise." The angels of praise are said to be members of the choir of Thrones.

See *ministering angels, Thrones.*

Pravuil: According to the Second Book of Enoch, Pravuil is an Archangel who keeps the celestial records. This includes all the activities and sayings of God, as well as lists of everyone who has ever lived. According to Enoch, God said to Pravuil: "Sit and write all the souls of Mankind, however many of them are born, and the places prepared for them to eternity; for all souls are prepared to eternity, before the formation of the world" (2 Enoch: 22–23).

Prayer, Angels of: The angels of prayer are special angels who have the task—and privilege—of delivering the prayers of exemplary human beings to the Throne of God. The people who receive this special treatment are holy, worthy, spiritual beings whose lives demonstrate they are performing the work of God. There are possibly seven angels of prayer, as the Archangels listed by Pseudo-Dionysius are all said to bring special prayers to the attention of God. They are: Chamuel, Gabriel, Jophiel, Michael, Raphael, Uriel, and Zadkiel. Other angels who may also be angels of prayer are: Akatriel, Metatron, Orifiel, Sandalphon, Simiel, Sizouse, and Zachariel.

See *Archangels,* individual angels, *Throne of God.*

Preceptor Angels: According to the Jewish Kabbalah, all of the great patriarchs had a special guardian angel. Examples include:

Adam: Raziel
Shem: Jophiel
Noah: Zaphkiel
Abraham: Zadkiel
Isaac: Raphael
Joseph, Joshua, and Daniel: Gabriel
Jacob: Peliel

Moses: Metatron

Elijah: Malashiel (Elijah later became Sandalphon.)

Samson: Camael

David: Cerviel

Solomon: Michael

See *guardian angels*, individual angels.

Pregnant Angel: People are always surprised when I mention a pregnant angel, and they assure me that it's not possible. Yet, in The Revelation of St. John the Divine we read: "And there appeared a great wonder in Heaven; a woman clothed with the sun, and the moon under her feet, and upon her head a crown of twelve stars. And she being with child cried, travailing in birth, and pained to be delivered" (12:1–2). Over the years, various suggestions have been made about the meaning of this pregnant angel. I've been told it symbolizes the Virgin Mary giving birth to Jesus. Another suggestion says the woman symbolizes Heaven, and the baby represents God's kingdom waiting to be born. Of course, it may simply be a pregnant angel.

Presence, Angels of the: The Angels of the Presence are a select group of angels who, according to the Book of Jubilees, were created on the first day. They have the immense privilege of living in the presence of God. The Angels of the Presence are sometimes called Elohim and are sometimes referred to as "the angels of the face." In Judaism, there were twelve Angels of the Presence. In Christianity, the number of angels considered Angels of the Presence ranges from seven to seventy. Most authorities think there are probably twelve. Different angels have been suggested for this most important task. The angels who are usually named are: Akatriel, Astanphaeus, Jehoel, Metatron, Michael, Phanuel, Saraqael, Uriel, Yefifiyyah, and Zagzagel. Melchizedek, Sandalphon, and Sariel are also frequently considered Angels of the Presence.

See *Elohim*, individual angels.

Principalities (Princes): The Principalities are the seventh-highest ranked angels in Dionysius' hierarchy of angels. They guide and assist leaders, rulers, and nations. They also assist religions in spreading the truth and supervise the rise and fall of nations. They oversee the work of the guardian angels. The chiefs of the choir of Principalities include Amael, Anael, and Cerviel. Artists depict the Principalities wearing armor and a crown. The crown symbolizes the name "prince." They usually carry a cross, a scepter, or a sword.

See *Amael, Anael, Cerviel, Dionysius the Areopagite, guardian angels, hierarchy of angels.*

Pronoia: In the Gnostic tradition, Pronoia was an archon who helped God create Adam. Apparently, Pronoia supplied the nerve tissue.

See *Adam, archons.*

Punishment, Angels of: There are several known angels of punishment. Most perform their duties in Hell, but Moses met five of them in Heaven. The best known ones are: Amaliel, Hutriel, Kushiel, Lahatiel, Makatiel, Puriel, Rogziel, and Shoftiel.

See *Lahatiel, Puriel.*

Puriel (Puruel or Pusiel): Puriel is an Angel of Punishment. He examines every soul that enters Heaven to ensure they meet his high standards. He is said to be ruthless in dealing with the wicked.

See *punishment (angels of).*

Qaddism (Kadishim): "Holy Ones." In Jewish lore, the qaddism are two commanding angels who stand with the watchers on either side of the Throne of God. One watcher and one holy one stand on each side of the throne, facing God. They guard and serve God, and also serve as his legal advisors, debating and judging every issue that comes to God's throne. The two qaddism are said to be twins. Although they are not named, they are said to possess seventy names each. The number seventy relates to the seventy nations and seventy languages spoken in the pre-Christian world. The qaddism are important angels in Heaven and are senior members of the Sarim.

See *Sarim, Throne of God, watchers.*

Queen of Angels: In the Kaballah, the Shekinah is considered the Queen of Angels. In Gnosticism, the Queen of Angels is Pistis Sophia. Pope Pius XII conferred the title Queen of Angels (*regina angelium*) to the Virgin Mary in 1954. (The Roman Catholic Church also calls her Angel of Peace and the Queen of Apostles,

confessors, Earth, Heaven, patriarchs, prophets, and saints.) However, the Virgin Mary has been known by this title since the ninth
century, when she may even have been more popular than her
son, Jesus. In the Middle Ages, people believed that the Virgin
Mary did not die but was taken up to Heaven while she was still
alive. In her role as Queen of Angels, Mary acts as a mediator
between God and humankind.

See *Shekinah, Sophia.*

Quelamia: According to the Book of Raziel (part of the Kabbalah),
Quelamia is one of the seven important angels who surround the
Throne of God.

See *Throne of God.*

Questioning the Dead: In Islam, there are two angels, Munkar and
Nakir, who question the recently dead in order to decide if their
souls should go to Heaven or Hell. People who give the correct
answers are given instant access to Paradise. The unfortunate people who give the wrong answers are left outside the gates of Hell.

See *Munkar, Nakir.*

Ra'amiel: "Trembling Before God." According to the Third Book of Enoch, Ra'amiel belongs to the Rulers of the Earth and is responsible for thunder. He frequently works with Matariel, another angel from the same group, who is in charge of rain.

See *Matariel, Rulers of the Earth.*

Ra'ashiel: According to the Third Book of Enoch, Ra'ashiel belongs to the Rulers of the Earth and is responsible for earthquakes.

See *Rulers of the Earth.*

Racheil (Rachiel): Racheil belongs to the choir of Ophanim and is the ruler of the planet Venus. Because of Venus' association with love and sexuality, Racheil can be invoked for help in these areas. See *Ophanim.*

Rachmiel: Rachmiel is one of the angels of mercy. He is also sometimes invoked for help during childbirth.

Raglueriel (Radweriel): Radueriel is described in the Third Book of Enoch as the celestial archivist, and he is believed to be the wisest angel in Heaven. He is also leader of the heavenly choirs, and is said to be a prince of the Sarim, which makes him an extremely important angel. Some sources say he is more important than Metatron. Radueriel is important in another way, also. Apparently, according to the Talmud, every time Radueriel says something, a new angel is created. He is the only angel in the entire celestial kingdom with this God-given ability. Radueriel is also the angel of poetry and can be invoked whenever you seek wisdom or insight.

See *Metatron, Sarim.*

Raguel (Phanael, Raguil, or Ragael): "Friend of God." Raguel supervises the behavior of his fellow angels and is Ruler of the Order of Dominions, a member of the Sarim, the angel of penance, and guardian of the Second Heaven. The Second Heaven is ruled by Raphael, and it is where the fallen angels are confined until Judgment Day. Raguel is often considered an Archangel. According to the Second Book of Enoch, Raguel and Sariel are the two angels who brought Enoch to Heaven. At the council in Rome in 745 CE, Pope Zachary demoted several angels, including Adimus, Inias, Raguel, Sabaoth, Simiel, Tubuas, and Uriel. They are known as reprobated angels. Raguel is considered a kind, caring assistant to God. You should call on Raguel if you are trying to affirm or strengthen your faith.

See *Archangels, Dominions, Enoch, fallen angels,* individual angels, *reprobated angels, Sarim.*

Rahab: Rahab is the angel of the sea. According to Jewish legend, God commanded Rahab to drink enough of the sea to create land suitable for mankind to live on. Rahab was happy with water covering the world, and so refused. God was furious at this disobedience and personally destroyed him. There is a possible allusion to this in the Bible: "Awake, awake, put on strength, O arm of the Lord; awake, as in the ancient days, in the generations of old. Art thou not it that hath cut Rahab, and wounded the dragon?" (Isaiah 51:9). Rahab's rotting body caused such an incredible stench that God sank it to the bottom of the sea, where it still possesses a foul odor.

That should have been the end of Rahab, but he figures in other legends as well. Apparently, he tried to prevent the Hebrews from crossing the parted Red Sea. This meant God had to kill him again.

Rahab partially redeemed himself by finding the Book of the Angel Raziel that Raziel had given to Adam. Jealous angels tried to prevent Adam from reading this book and learning its secrets. They stole the book and threw it into the sea, but Rahab recovered it and returned it to Adam. Because of this, people who have lost valuable items at sea sometimes invoke Rahab for help.

See *Raziel*.

Rahatiel (Rahtiel): According to Jewish tradition, Rahatiel is one of the Rulers of the Earth and is responsible for looking after the constellations and the stars. According to the Third Book of Enoch, Metatron named all the stars for Rabbi Ishmael and Rahatiel "entered them in counted order" (3 Enoch 46).

See *Enoch (Book of)*, *Metatron*, *Rulers of the Earth*.

Rahmiel (Ra'amiel or Rhamiel): Rahmiel and Raphael are the two angels of mercy, compassion, and love. Rahmiel can be called upon to help people who lack love and compassion. Rahmiel's main task is to encourage empathy, kindness, compassion, and understanding throughout the world. Some people believe that when St. Francis died, he became the angel Rahmiel. Enoch, Elijah, St. Anne (the mother of the Virgin Mary), St. Francis of Assisi, and Moroni are the only other humans who may have been transformed into angels. This is called angelification. Enoch became Metatron, Elijah became Sandalphon, Jacob became Uriel, and St. Anne became Anas.

As Ra'amiel, Rahmiel belongs to the Rulers of the Earth and is responsible for thunder.

See *angelification, Metatron, Moroni, Raphael, Rulers of the Earth, Sandalphon, Uriel.*

Raman: Raman is the yazata angel in Zoroastrianism who is responsible for joy and happiness.

See *yazata, Zoroastrianism.*

Ramiel: See *Remiel.*

Raphael (Re-fa-el): "God Heals." Raphael is one of the most important Archangels. Raphael is considered Regent of the Sun, Ruler of the Second Heaven, Chief of the Order of Virtues, and a member of the influential Sarim. He is also a member of the Seraphim, Cherubim, and Dominions. Another of his tasks is to look after the Tree of Life in the Garden of Eden. Raphael has a special interest in healing, creativity, knowledge, science, communication, travel, and young people. Raphael has been considered head of the guardian angels since he acted as Tobias' guardian in the Book of Tobit. Raphael is sometimes called the angel of compassion, and he demonstrated his healing ability by curing Tobit's blindness. He also removed the pain Abraham suffered after his circumcision and is believed to be the angel who healed Jacob's thigh after his fight with an angel (Genesis 32:24–31). In addition, some accounts say he either taught Noah about medicine or gave him a book on the subject to take with him on the ark. Legend says this was the Book of the Angel Raziel. When Solomon prayed to God, asking for help in building his Great Temple, God ordered Raphael to deliver a pentagram ring to Solomon. This ring enabled Solomon to force the demons to work on the temple and get it finished.

In addition to healing people and looking after the guardian angels, Raphael is also engaged in healing the earth. In effect, Raphael is the guardian angel of humanity. Raphael is associated with the sun and has an excellent sense of humor. Artists normally depict Raphael as a traveller, holding a staff and a fish. According to tradition, Raphael was originally called Labbiel.

See *Archangels, Cherubim, demon, Dominions, guardian angels, Labbiel, Raziel, Sarim, Seraphim.*

Rapithwin: Rapithwin is a yazata angel in the Zoroastrian tradition. He looks after the hours from noon until 3 PM, and he is known as Lord of the Noonday Heat. Rapithwin is important, as it is his gentle warmth that enables crops to grow. During the winter months, he ensures the roots of plants do not freeze.

See *yazata, Zoroastrianism.*

Rasanstat: Rasanstat is a female yazata angel in Zoroastrianism. She encourages truth and honesty in all undertakings.

See *yazata, Zoroastrianism.*

Rashnu (Rashin): Rashnu is the yazata angel of justice in Zoroastrianism. He stands in front of the bridge that connects earth and Heaven, and, with the help of Mithra and Sraosha, weighs the souls of all newly deceased people. This process takes three days. If the person passes this test, a beautiful woman escorts him or her into Heaven. If the person fails the test, he or she can still cross the bridge but will face an alarming sequence of grisly horrors as the bridge grows narrower. Finally, the person is cut to shreds by the razor-like metal of the bridge and falls down to Hell.

See *Mithra, Sraosha, yazata, Zoroastrianism.*

Rata: Rata is the female yazata angel in Zoroastrianism who encourages charity and helpfulness.

See *yazata, Zoroastrianism.*

Raziel: "Secret of God." Raziel is the wise angel who apparently felt sorry for Adam and Eve when they were banished from the Garden of Eden and so gave Adam the Book of the Angel Raziel. This book contained all the knowledge of the universe and enabled Adam to make a life for himself outside the garden (see *Rahab*). After Adam's death, the book was eventually found by Enoch, who memorized it and became the wisest man of his time. Later still, it came into the hands of Noah, who used it to help build his ark. Hundreds of years later, the book belonged to King Solomon, who used it to create magic. Unfortunately, after his death, the book disappeared. (Although this is a good story, a Jewish scholar probably wrote the Book of the Angel Raziel in the Middle Ages.)

Raziel is said to be a member of the Cherubim, and he has a strong interest in magic and knowledge. He is also a prince of the choir of Thrones, chief of the Erelim, and a member of the Sarim. You should contact Raziel whenever you need answers to imponderable questions. Raziel particularly enjoys helping original thinkers develop their ideas. Raziel is said to have blue wings and an intense yellow aura around his head. He wears a gray robe, which appears to be liquid, rather than solid.

See *Cherubim, Enoch, Erelim, Rahab, Sarim, Thrones*.

Rehael (Ray-ha-el): Rehael belongs to the choir of Powers and is the angel of longevity. Rehael is one of the seventy-two Schemhamphoras, a group of angels who bear the various names of God found in Jewish scriptures. Rehael is the angel of self-respect, and works tirelessly to inspire respect for one's parents. He also works hard to promote humanitarian ideals. Rehael works with both the mind and the body, promoting health. Rehael can be invoked for health matters, self-respect, and respect for others (especially parents). Rehael is guardian angel for people born between October 4 and 8.

See *guardian angels, Powers, Schemhamphoras*.

Rejajel (Ray-ya-yel) **(Reiiel or Reiyel):** Rejajel belongs to the choir of Dominions and is one of the seventy-two Schemhamphoras, a group of angels who bear the various names of God found in Jewish scriptures. He is guardian angel for people born between

August 13 and 17. People who are thinking ahead and making long-term plans can call upon him for help and advice.

See *Dominions, guardian angels, Schemhamphoras*.

Remiel (Ramiel, Eremiel, or Jeremiel): Remiel is the angel of divine vision. He is one of the seven Archangels who attend the Throne of God. Remiel has the task of looking after the souls of the faithful once Michael has weighed them. He is happy to help people with a particular need to see into the future.

See *Archangels, Michael, Throne of God*.

Reprobated Angels: In 745 CE, Pope Zachary convened a church council to discuss the increasing popularity of angels. The authorities were concerned that people were starting to worship angels rather than God (angelolatry). As a result of this council, only the three angels mentioned by name in the Bible—Michael, Gabriel, and Raphael—were considered worthy of veneration. Seven important angels were reprobated, which means they were considered inauthentic by the church authorities. These were: Adimus, Inias, Raguel, Saboac, Simiel, Tubuas, and Uriel. Pope Zachary described Raguel as a demon who "passed himself off as a saint."

See *angelolatry, demon*, individual angels.

Requiel: Requiel is one of the twenty-eight angels who govern the mansions of the moon. Requiel is in charge of Zabadola, the twenty-third mansion. In this role, he helps sick people regain their health. He also helps prisoners gain their freedom and encourages unhappy couples to divorce.

See *mansions of the moon*.

Ridwan: In the Islamic tradition, Ridwan is the angel who stands at the entrance to Heaven. His task is to protect and guard Paradise.

Rikbiel (Rikbiel YHWH): Rikbiel is a member of the choir of Cherubim, Prince of the Merkabah, and a member of the Sarim. He is also leader of the order of Galgallim. Although not much is known about Rikbiel, in Enochian lore he is considered to be even more important than Metatron in Heaven.

See *Cherubim, Galgallim, Merkabah, Metatron, Sarim.*

Rochel (Ro-shel) **(Roehel):** Rochel is the angel of lost property and can be invoked when anything is misplaced or lost. Rochel is also the guardian angel of people born between March 1 and 5. As Roehel, he is one of the seventy-two Schemhamphoras, a group of angels who bear the various names of God found in Jewish scriptures.

See *guardian angels, Schemhamphoras.*

Rubiel: Rubiel is known as the gamblers' friend, and he is frequently invoked by people participating in games of chance. Gamblers also ask Barachiel and Uriel for luck and success.

See *Barachiel, Uriel.*

Ruchiel: In the Third Book of Enoch, Ruchiel is listed as one of the Rulers of the Earth. His responsibility is the wind.

See *Rulers of the Earth.*

Rulers of the Earth: The Third Book of Enoch lists eighteen angels who are responsible for the weather or the planets. Some of these, such as Ziqiel, ruler of sparks, might sound strange to us today, but they were considered important during the time of Enoch. The Rulers of the Earth are:

> Baradiel (Barchiel): Ruler of hail
> Baraqiel (Barchiel): Ruler of lightning
> Gabriel: Ruler of fire
> Galgalliel: Ruler of the sun
> Kokbiel (Kokabel): Ruler of the planets
> Lailiel: Ruler of the night
> Matariel: Ruler of rain
> 'Ophanniel (Ophaniel): Ruler of the moon
> Ra'amiel: Ruler of thunder

Ra'ashiel: Ruler of earthquakes

Rahatiel: Ruler of the constellations and the stars

Ruchiel: Ruler of the wind

Shalgiel: Ruler of snow

Shimshiel: Ruler of the day

Za'amiel: Ruler of vehemence

Za'aphiel: Ruler of storm wind

Zi'iel: Ruler of commotion

Ziqiel: Ruler of sparks

See individual angels.

Ruman: Ruman is the angel in the Islamic tradition who greets sinners when they first reach Hell. He ensures they write down every sin they have ever committed and then passes them on to Munkar and Nakir.

See *Islam (angels of)*, *Munkar, Nakir*.

Sabaoc: Sabaoc is one of the angels who were demoted at the Council of Rome in 745 CE. Pope Zachary became concerned at the public interest in angels and declared a number of them could no longer be venerated. These angels, known as the reprobated angels, are: Adimus, Inias, Raguel, Sabaoc, Simiel, Tubuas, and Uriel.

See individual angels, *reprobated angels*.

Sabath: Sabath is one of the two angels who rule the Sixth Heaven. He rules the daytime hours, and Zebul rules during the night.

See *Heavens, Zebul*.

Sabathiel: In the Jewish Kabbalah, Sabathiel is the angel responsible for the planet Saturn.

Sabbath, Angel of the: In Jewish lore, the Angel of the Sabbath is a highly ranked angel who was enthroned before God on the seventh day of Creation. The Angel of the Sabbath also helped

Adam when he was forced to leave the garden of Eden by asking God not to send Adam to Hell.

See *Adam*.

Sabrael: See *Sidriel*.

Sachiel: "Covering of God." Sachiel is considered the Archangel of Jupiter and is a member of the choir of Cherubim. Jupiter is the ruling planet of Sagittarius, and because of this, Sachiel provides support for Sagittarians. He has an interest in legal matters, good fortune, expansion, and beneficence. He is often invoked on financial matters. Sachiel is willing to help you earn money, but he will not help you obtain money for nothing. The Essenes, a religious sect who were active one hundred years before and after the life of Jesus, considered Sachiel to be the angel of water Sachiel and Zadkiel might be two names for the same angel.

See *Archangels, Cherubim, Zadkiel*.

Sagnessagiel (Sasnigiel): Sagnessagiel is the Prince of Wisdom. He provides wisdom, knowledge, and understanding. He teaches patience and forgiveness. It is possible that Sagnessagiel is another name for Metatron.

See *Metatron*.

Sahaqiel (Sa-ha-kee-yel) **(Sahaqi'el):** Sahaqiel is listed in the Third Book of Enoch as one of the seven great Archangels. He is also in charge of the Fourth Heaven and has 496,000 angels to attend and serve him.

See *Archangels*.

Salaphiel (Salatheel or Salathiel): "Communicant of God." Salaphiel is listed as one of the seven ministering Archangels in the Book of Tobit and the Book of Esdras. According to the Book of Adam and Eve, Salaphiel and Suriel brought Adam and Eve down from a mountaintop that Satan had lured them to, and they then took the pair to a cave of treasures. Salaphiel's main task is to help people pray. You can call on him for help if you want to learn how to pray more effectively.

See *Archangels, Satan, Suriel.*

Salem: Salem was the guardian angel of St. John.

See *guardian angels.*

Samael (Sammael or Samil): Samael was originally thought of as the Angel of Death and was considered an evil angel in Judaism. *Samael* means "blind god." In this sense, "blind" means ignorant, and the Gnostics considered ignorance to be the seat of evil. Because of this, Samael is sometimes considered a fallen angel. There is an alternative reason for Samael's name, "blind god." When Moses died, he was reluctant to give up his soul. Samael was sent to retrieve it, and Moses hurt him so badly with his staff that Samael became blind. God sent Gabriel, Michael, and Zagzagel to help Samael retrieve Moses' soul.

Samael is reputed to have twelve wings, and he is covered with precious stones and crystals. Although Samael lives in the Seventh Heaven, he is in charge of the Fifth Heaven. He is one of the planetary angels and rules the planet Mars. Today, Samael is considered a protective angel who provides persistence and courage whenever necessary. Samael is willing to help you deal with your enemies in a gentle manner, enabling you to defuse and eliminate long-lasting difficulties. Rudolf Steiner considered Samael to be one of the seven great Archangels.

See *Archangels, death (angel of), fallen angels, Gabriel, Lahash, Michael, planetary angels, Steiner (Rudolf), Zagzagel.*

Samandiriel: According to Manichaean mythology, Samandiriel is the angel of fertility. Anyone having problems with conception can invoke Samandiriel for help. Samandiriel can also be called upon on any matter concerning imagination, visualization, and creativity.

Samaqiel (Semeqiel or Samquiel): Samaqiel is the angel of Capricorn and helps Archangel Anael look after people born under this sign.

See *Anael, Archangels.*

Samrafil: Samrafil is an angel in the Islamic tradition. When Muhammad and Archangel Gabriel toured the seven Heavens, they continued on as far as the Lote-Tree of the Furthest Boundary. Beyond this point there is absolute nothingness. The Lote-Tree is an indescribable tree, so large that it covers all the Heavens and universes. Each branch of the tree is five hundred thousand light-years away from the next branch. The trunk of this tree is an enormous angel called Samrafil. A huge angel also sits on every leaf of the Lote-Tree.

See *Archangels, Gabriel.*

Sandalphon (Sandalfon): Sandalphon is an Archangel, the head of the guardian angels, and—according to some sources—one of the Angels of the Presence. Sandalphon assists Metatron to weave Jewish prayers into garlands for God to wear on his head. Despite his preference for Jewish prayers, Sandalphon is willing to carry any prayer to Heaven. According to Jewish legend, Sandalphon was originally the prophet Elijah and is considered Metatron's twin brother. According to the Bible, "Elijah went up by a whirlwind into Heaven" (2 Kings 2:11). Sandalphon is extremely tall, and it is believed that it would take five hundred years to climb from his feet to the top of his head. Sandalphon is also in charge of bird life, and he is always portrayed with a number of birds flying around him. Sandalphon usually has a sword close by, as one of his tasks is to help Michael fight Satan. In the Kabbalah, Sandalphon is considered the Archangel of Malkuth.

See *Archangels, guardian angels, Metatron, Presence (Angels of the).*

Sansenoy (Sansanui, Sanvi, or Sansennoi): In Jewish tradition, Sansenoy and two other angels, Senoy and Semangelof, brought Adam's first wife, Lilith, back to him. However, the marriage did not last, and Adam finally rejected her. Lilith became a demon who preyed on pregnant women and young children. Pregnant women used to wear amulets engraved with Sansenoy's name to protect them from Lilith.

See *Lilith, Semangelof, Senoy.*

Santriel: Santriel is mentioned in the Zohar as the angel who collects the bodies of men and women who failed to honor the Sabbath while they were alive. The bodies are taken to Gehenna and shown to other sinners as a warning.

Sapiel: "Wisdom of God." Saint Umiltà of Faenzà (1226–1310) had two guardian angels, Sapiel and Emmanuel. These angels became her closest friends and confidantes. Sapiel is incredibly beautiful and wears a coat containing every color imaginable. He also wears numerous gemstones.

See *Emmanuel, guardian angels.*

Saraqael (Sarakiel): Saraqael is considered an Archangel in the First Book of Enoch. He is also sometimes listed as an Angel of the Presence. Some authorities think Saraqael is another name for Uriel.

See *Archangels, Presence (Angels of the), Uriel.*

Sarasael: Sarasael is known for telling Noah that the vine Satan had planted in the Garden of Eden to deceive Adam and Eve had been washed out of Paradise by the Great Flood. According to the Third Book of Baruch, Sarasael told Noah to replant the vine and look after it, as in time the wine produced from the grapes would be transubstantiated into the blood of Christ, in the same way that Jesus' sacrifice would ultimately enable humankind to return to Paradise.

Sariel: "God's Command." According to the Book of Enoch, Sariel was one of the original seven Archangels. Sariel is one of the Angels of the Presence and a member of the Sarim. He and Raguel are the two angels who took Enoch up to Heaven. Sariel helps people who want to learn. In Hebrew lore, Sariel encouraged Moses to study. He is also interested in healing and assists Raphael in this work. Sariel provides guidance whenever it is needed. He is frequently invoked in ceremonial magic and provides protection against the evil eye. Sariel looks after people born under the sign of Aries. One unusual facet of Sariel is that he sometimes manifests himself as an ox.

See *Archangels, Enoch, Presence (Angels of the), Raguel, Raphael, Sarim.*

Sarim: The Sarim are the Angel Princes in Heaven. They constantly sing the praises of God. The word *sarim* comes from the Hebrew *sar*, which means "prince." The Sarim are led by Tagas and are responsible for looking after Heaven and earth. Members of the Sarim include some of the most powerful angels in Heaven: Akatriel, Anael, Anafiel, Azbuga, Barchiel, Chamuel, Chayyiel, Gabriel, Galgaliel, The Irin, Jehoel, Jophiel, Metatron, Michael, The Qaddism, Radweriel, Raguel, Raphael, Raziel, Rikbiel, Sandalphon, Sariel, Shemuil, Sopheriel Mehayye, Sopheriel Memeth, Soqed Hozi, Uriel, Yefefiah, Zadkiel, and Zagzagel.

See individual angels, *Tagas.*

Saritaiel (Saritiel or Sairitaiel): Saritaiel is the angel of Sagittarius and helps Archangel Adnachiel look after people born under this sign.

See *Adnachiel, Archangels.*

Satan: Satan is leader of the fallen angels and the ultimate symbol of evil. The name *Satan* means "adversary" in Hebrew. Satan is known by many names, including Beelzebub, God of the Underworld, Lucifer, Mephistopheles, Prince of Darkness, and the devil.

In The Revelation of St. John the Divine, he is called the "great dragon" (Revelation 12:3; 12:7–9). He has his share of nicknames, as well. Examples include: "the bogeyman," "Evil One," "Jack Flash," "Old Hairy," "Old Horny," and "Old Red." According to Jewish tradition, Satan's name before the Fall was Satanael (not the same angel as Sataniel). The *el* means "God" in Hebrew, signifying Satanael's close relationship with God. After he fell, he naturally lost the privilege of having *el* at the end of his name.

Originally, Satan was one of God's finest and most beautiful angels. He thought so highly of himself that he wanted to be worshiped as a god. Satan's pride would not allow him to bow down before Adam. By refusing God's command, Satan became the first angel to sin. Having crossed this line, Satan and many other angels—possibly as many as a third of the angels in Heaven—declared war on God. Not surprisingly, they were soundly defeated and became fallen angels. Since then, Satan and his followers have lived in Hell, where they endlessly wage war on the righteous.

One of Satan's plots involved Adam and Eve. Satan turned himself into a serpent and tricked Eve into disobeying the word of God. He accused God of lying to the young couple, and said he had held back information from them. One Jewish legend says Satan seduced Eve, and that Cain, the first murderer, was the result of this union.

Satan has been trying to lead people into the path of wickedness ever since he was cast out of Heaven. One extreme example of this is when he showed Jesus all the kingdoms in the world and said, "All these things will I give thee, if thou wilt fall down and worship me" (Matthew 4:9; Luke 4:5–7).

Satan is called Iblis in Islam, and they also consider him to be the devil, as he refused to bow down and worship Adam. In Zoroastrianism, the devil is called Angra Mainya.

See *Angra Mainya, devil, dragon, fallen angels, Iblis, Jesus.*

Sataniel: Sataniel is one of the ruling angels of the zodiac and is responsible for the sign of Cancer.

See *zodiac (angels of the)*.

Sayitziel (Saitziel): Sayitziel is the angel of Scorpio and helps Archangel Barchiel look after people born under this sign.

See *Archangels, Barchiel*.

Scheliel: Scheliel is one of the twenty-eight angels who govern the mansions of the moon. He is responsible for Aldimiach, the seventh mansion. Scheliel helps friends and lovers and people engaged in making a profit. However, he also works against people in authority.

See *mansions of the moon*.

Schemhamphoras (Shemhamphorae): The Schemhamphoras are a group of seventy-two angels who bear the various names of God found in Jewish scriptures. The first mention of this is in the Bible: "Behold, I send an Angel before thee, to keep thee in the way, and to bring thee into the place which I have prepared. Beware of him, and obey his voice, provoke him not; for he will not pardon your trangressions: for my name is in him" (Exodus 23:20–21). These names are believed to possess magical power, and they were, and still are, invoked by magicians. The Egyptians were the first to devise names that could be used for magical purposes, but the Greeks, Assyrians, and Hebrews were all aware of the immense power that can be created by vibrations of sound. By far the most powerful name is the Tetragrammaton, which is the sacred name of God. It is normally written as YHVH, and is pronounced "Yahweh," and sometimes written as YHWH. However, because this name is so sacred, it was rarely ever pronounced. The Schemhamphora angels are also sometimes considered guardian angels.

Here are the seventy-two Schemhamphoras and the verses from Jewish scriptures associated with them:

1. Vehujah: Thou, O Lord, art my guardian, and exaltest my head.

2. Ieliel: Do not remove thy help from me, O Lord, and look to my defence.

3. Sirael: I shall say so to the Lord, Thou art my guardian, my God is my refuge, and I shall hope in him.

4. Elemijel: Turn, O Lord, and deliver my soul, and save me for Thy mercy's sake.

5. Lelahel: Let him who lives in Zion sing unto the Lord, and proclaim his goodwill among the peoples.

6. Achajah: The Lord is merciful and compassionate, long-suffering and of great goodness.

7. Mahasiah: I called upon the Lord and he heard me and delivered me from all my tribulations.

8. Cahatel: O come let us adore and fall down before God who bore us.

9. Haziel: Remember Thy mercies, O Lord, and Thy mercies which have been forever.

10. Aladiah: Perform thy mercies upon us, for we have hoped in Thee.

11. Laviah: The Lord liveth, blessed is my God, and let the God of my salvation be exalted.

12. Hahajah (1 of 2): Why hast Thou departed, O Lord, so long from us, perishing in the times of tribulation.

13. Jezalel: Rejoice in the Lord, all ye lands, sing, exult, and play upon a stringed instrument.

14. Mebahel: The Lord is a refuge, and my God the help of my hope.

15. Hariel: The Lord is a refuge for me, and my God the help of my hope.

16. Hakamiah: O Lord, God of my salvation, by day have I called to thee, and sought Thy presence by night.

17. Leviah: O Lord our Lord, How wonderful is Thy name in all the world.

18. Caliel: Judge me, O Lord, according to Thy loving kindness, and let not them be joyful over me, O Lord.

19. Lauviah: I waited in hope for the Lord, and He turned to me.

20. Pahaliah: I shall call upon the name of the Lord, O Lord, free my soul.

21. Nelakhel: In Thee also have I hoped, O Lord, and said, Thou art my God.

22. Jajajel: The Lord keep thee, the Lord be thy protection O Thy right hand.

23. Melahel: The Lord keep thine incoming and thine outgoing from this time forth for evermore.

24. Hahajah (2 of 2): The Lord is well pleased with those that fear Him and hope upon his mercy.

25. Haajah: I have called upon Thee with all my heart and shall tell forth all Thy wonders.

26. Nithhaja: I shall acknowledge Thee, O Lord, with all my heart, hear me, O Lord, and I shall seek my justification.

27. Jerathel: Save me, O Lord, from the evil man and deliver me from the wicked doer.

28. Sehijah: Let not God depart from me, look to my help, O God.

29. Rejajel: Behold, God is my helper, and the Lord is the guardian of my soul.

30. Omael: For Thou art my strength, O Lord. O Lord, Thou art my hope from my youth.

31. Lecabel: I shall enter into the power of the Lord, my God, I shall be mindful of Thy justice only.

32. Vasariah: For the word of the Lord is upright, and all His works faithful.

33. Jehuvajah: The Lord knows the thoughts of men, for they are in vain.

34. Lehahiah: Let Israel hope in the Lord from this time forth and for evermore.

35. Chavakiah: I am joyful, for the Lord hears the voice of my prayer.
36. Manadel: I have delighted in the beauty of Thy house, O Lord, and in the place of the habitation of Thy glory.
37. Aniel: O Lord God, turn thy power towards us, and show us Thy face and we shall be saved.
38. Haamiah: For Thou art my hope, O Lord, and Thou hast been my deepest refuge.
39. Rehael: The Lord has heard me and pitied me and the Lord is my helper.
40. Ihiazel: Why drivest Thou away my soul, O Lord, and turnest thy face from me?
41. Hahahel: O Lord, deliver my soul from wicked lips and a deceitful tongue.
42. Michael (1 of 2): The Lord protects thee from all evil and will protect thy soul.
43. Vevaliah: I have cried unto Thee, O Lord, and let my prayer come unto Thee.
44. Ielahiah: Make my wishes pleasing unto Thee, O Lord, and teach me Thy judgments.
45. Sealiah: If I say that my foot is moved, Thou wilt help me of Thy mercy.
46. Ariel: The Lord is pleasant to all the world and His mercies are over all His works.
47. Asaliah: How wonderful are Thy works, O Lord, and how deep Thy thoughts.
48. Michael (2 of 2): The Lord hath made thy salvation known in the sight of the peoples and will reveal His justice.
49. Vehael: Great is the Lord and worthy to be praised, and there is no end to his greatness.
50. Daniel: The Lord is pitiful and merciful, long-suffering and of great goodness.

51. Hahasiah: Let the Lord be in glory forever and the Lord will rejoice in His works.

52. Imamiah: I shall make known the Lord, according to His justice, and sing hymns to the name of the Lord, the greatest.

53. Nanael: I have known Thee, O Lord, for Thy judgments are just, and in Thy truth have I abased myself.

54. Nithael: The Lord hath prepared His seat in Heaven and His rule shall be over all.

55. Mebahiah: Thou remainest for ever, O Lord, and Thy memorial is from generation to generation.

56. Polial: The Lord raiseth up all who fall and setteth up the broken.

57. Nemamiah: They who fear the Lord have hoped in the Lord, He is their helper and their protector.

58. Jejalel: My soul is greatly troubled, but Thou, O Lord are here also.

59. Harahel: From the rising of the Sun to the going down of the same, the word of the Lord is worthy to be praised.

60. Mizrael: The Lord is just in all his ways and blessed in all his works.

61. Umbael: Let the name of the Lord be blessed from this time for evermore.

62. Iahael: See, O Lord, how I have delighted in Thy commandments according to Thy life-giving mercy.

63. Anaviel: Serve ye the Lord with gladness and enter into His sight with exultation.

64. Mehikiel: Behold the eyes of the Lord are upon those that fear Him and hope in His loving kindness.

65. Damabiah: Turn, O Lord, even here also, and be pleased with Thy servants.

66. Meniel: Neither leave me, Lord, nor depart from me.

67. Ejael: Delight in the Lord and He will give thee petitions of thy heart.

68. Habujah: Confess to the Lord, for He is God, and His mercy is forever.
69. Roehel: The Lord is my inheritance and my cup and it is Thou who restorest mine inheritance.
70. Jabamiah: In the beginning, God created the Heaven and the earth.
71. Hajael: I shall confess to the Lord with my mouth and praise Him in the midst of the multitude.
72. Mumijah: Return to thy rest, my soul, for the Lord doeth thee good.

See *guardian angels*, individual angels, *Tetragrammaton*, *YHVH*.

Scotus, John Duns: John Duns Scotus (c.1266–1308) was a philosopher and theologian. He was known as "Doctor Subtilis" because of his talent at subtly merging opposing views. He was probably born in Duns, Scotland, and was ordained in Northampton, England, in 1291. He taught theology at universities in Paris, Oxford, and Cologne. He may have also taught at Cambridge University. John Scotus believed angels were made of "spiritual matter," and were "incorporeal and immaterial." He also believed angels possessed personalities and had individual quirks and characteristics. Consequently, they were similar to people, but slightly more evolved. This idea made angels much more approachable, a comforting thought to those who had been brought up learning about strict Old Testament angels.

Scribes: According to the Third Book of Enoch, the Scribes are an important order of angels. Their task is to record everyone's good and bad deeds and to read them out at the meetings of the celestial court.

Sealiah (Say-ah-lee-yah) **(Sehaliah or Seeliah):** Sealiah is one of the seventy-two Schemhamphoras, a group of angels who bear the various names of God found in Jewish scriptures. He is guardian angel of people born between November 3 and 7. He provides happiness and good health to people who ask for it.

See *guardian angels, Schemhamphoras.*

Sealtiel: "Request of God." Sealtiel has a special interest in meditation, contemplation, spirituality, and worship. Some authorities say he is an Archangel. It is possible he was the Angel of the Lord who stopped Abraham from sacrificing Isaac (Genesis 22:12). However, several other angels have also been suggested for this task.

See *Lord (Angel of the), Archangels.*

Seasonal Angels: The seasonal angels govern the four seasons.

Spring—Head angel: Spugliguel. Other angels: Amatiel, Caracasa, Core, and Commissoros.

Summer—Head angel: Tubiel. Other angels: Gargatel, Gaviel, and Tariel.

Autumn—Head angel: Torquaret. Other angels: Tarquam and Guabarel.

Winter—Head angel: Attarib. Other angels: Amabael and Ceterari.

Rudolf Steiner (1861–1925), the founder of Anthroposophy, associated the four main Archangels with the seasons: Raphael (Spring), Uriel (Summer), Michael (Autumn), and Gabriel (Winter).

See *Archangels, Gabriel, Michael, Raphael, Steiner (Rudolf), Uriel.*

Sedekiah: Sedekiah is frequently invoked by prospectors and people searching for hidden treasure, such as gold and diamonds.

Seheliel: Seheliel is an angel who helps people gain their desires. He also provides unlimited energy when necessary.

Sehijah (Say-hay-yah) **(Seheiah):** Sehijah is one of the seventy-two Schemhamphoras, a group of angels who bear the various names of God found in Jewish scriptures. Sehijah is the guardian angel for people born between August 7 and 12. Sehijah is a protective angel who looks after people when they're away from home.

See *guardian angels, Schemhamphoras.*

Semangelof: Semangelof, Sansenoy, and Senoy are the three angels who brought Adam's first wife, Lilith, back to him when she left. Lilith disliked Adam's authority and swore revenge on all the daughters of Eve who allow their husbands to rule and control them. Pregnant women and young children used to wear amulets inscribed with the Semangelof's name to protect them from Lilith.

See *Lilith, Sansenoy, Senoy.*

Semeliel (Semeschia): In the Jewish Kabbalah, Semeliel is the angel responsible for the sun. Cornelius Agrippa thought he was one of the seven mighty princes who stood before God.

Semyaza: See *Shemhazai.*

Senoy: Senoy, Sansenoy, and Semangelof are the three angels who were sent to return Lilith to her husband, Adam. Pregnant women and young children used to wear amulets inscribed with the Senoy's name to protect them from Lilith.

See *Lilith, Sansenoy, Semangelof.*

Seraph: A Seraph is a member of the choir of Seraphim. An immensely powerful light is emanated by Seraphs, making it impossible for people to look at them. When St. Francis of Assisi (c.1181–1226) received his stigmata in 1224, he became one of the few humans to see a Seraph.

See *Seraphim.*

Seraphiel (Serapiel): Seraphiel is one of the leaders of the Seraphim and teaches the other Seraphs how to sing the praises of God. He is the most important Merkabah angel, as he is one of the eight judgment throne angels. Seraphiel is said to have the face of an angel and the body of an eagle. Humans cannot invoke a Seraph, but it is possible to ask Seraphiel to provide contentment and peace of mind.

See *Merkabah, Seraphim.*

Seraphim: "The Burning Ones." The Seraphim are the highest-ranking of the nine choirs of angels, and they are the angels closest to God. They have four faces and six wings. According to some sources, their wings are a bright, luminous red. The best description of the Seraphim is found in the Bible: "Above it stood the seraphims: each one had six wings; with twain he covered his face, and with twain he covered his feet, and with twain he did fly. And one cried unto another, and said, Holy, holy, holy, is the Lord of hosts: the whole earth is full of his glory" (Isaiah 6:2–3). The Third Book of Enoch says the Seraphim have sixteen heads, four facing each cardinal direction. Their light is so strong that humans could not exist in their presence. Even fellow angels, including important ones such as the Cherubim, cannot look at them because their divine, flaming light is so powerful. This light consists of flames of divine, healing love. The Seraphim fly endlessly around the celestial throne singing, "Holy, Holy, Holy." Members of the Seraphim include: Chamuel, Jehoel, Metatron, Michael, Nathanael, Samael, and Seraphiel.

See *Cherubim, hierarchy of angels,* individual angels.

Serayel: Serayel is the angel of Gemini and helps Archangel Ambriel look after people born under this sign.

See *Ambriel, Archangels.*

Seven Heavens, Angels of: See *Heavens.*

Shalgiel (Salgiel): According to the Third Book of Enoch, Shalgiel is one of the Rulers of the Earth and is responsible for snow and blizzards.

See *Rulers of the Earth.*

Shamshiel (Shimshiel, Shamsiel, or Simsiel): "Light of Day." According to Jewish tradition, Shamshiel looks after the Garden of Eden. He gave Moses a guided tour of the garden. He is prepared to help anyone who has a genuine desire to improve his or her garden. According to the Third Book of Enoch, Shimshiel is one of the Rulers of the Earth and is responsible for daylight.

See *Rulers of the Earth*.

Sharahiel (Sharhiel): Sharahiel is the angel of the astrological sign of Aries. He helps Archangel Malkhidael look after the month of March.

See *Archangels, Malkhidael*.

Sharahil: In the Islamic tradition, Sharahil is the angel who looks after the nighttime hours. At sunset every day, he hangs a large black diamond on the western horizon. An angel called Harahil displays a large white diamond on the eastern horizon at dawn every day. Apparently, these two diamonds act together to ensure the proper rotation of the earth. They also ensure that day follows night.

See *Harahil*.

Shekinah, The: In Jewish tradition, the Shekinah is the feminine aspect of God. *Shekinah* means "shelter" or "dwelling place." She is the Great Mother of the universe, the Queen of Heaven, and the bride of God. She is believed to be the angel Jacob referred to as "The angel which redeemed me from all evil" (Genesis 48:16). Jewish mystics tell how the Shekinah was separated from her lover, God the Father, after Adam and Eve were expelled from the Garden of Eden. Ever since then, they have been together only on Friday nights, the night before the Sabbath. They will be reunited only when the original light of Creation returns to its source. Fortunately, every act of love, generosity, and compassion brings the couple closer together. The Shekinah provides unity and peace of mind, and delights in helping all lovers. In the Kaballah, the Shekinah is considered the Queen of Angels.

See *Queen of Angels*.

Shelachel (Malka Be-Tarshism Voed Ruachoth Shechalim): Shelachel is an angel of the moon and is believed to be similar in appearance to Archangel Gabriel.

See *Archangels, Gabriel.*

Shelathiel: Shelathiel is the angel of Virgo and helps Archangel Hamaliel look after people born under this sign.

See *Archangels, Hamaliel.*

Shemhazai (Shem-harts-eye) **(Semiaza, Semyaza, Shemjaza, or Shemyaza):** Shemhazai was the leader of the Grigori, the angels who came down to earth and had sexual relations with human women. Shemhazai fell in love with a young maiden called Istehar. She promised to give herself to him if he told her the secret name of God. However, once he told her the name, she said it and immediately ascended to Heaven. Because she was still pure, God placed her in the constellation of Pleiades, so mankind can always see her. Another version of this story says Shemhazai slept with Istehar and they produced two children who became Nephilim, the evil giants.

Angels of destruction were sent to kill the Nephilim, and Shemhazai became so upset that he flew up to the stars and into the constellation of Orion. He is still there, hanging upside down, halfway between Heaven and earth.

See *Grigori, Nephilim.*

Shemuil: Shemuil is an archon who attends to the prayers of Israel and ensures they reach the Seventh Heaven. Shemuil is also a member of the Sarim.

See *archons, Sarim.*

Shen: The shen are Chinese angels. Regarded as gods in China, they perform the same functions as angels. The shen were originally human, but have attained immortality and now spend their time helping people by providing strength, protection, healing, and instruction. They also exorcise demons. The shen normally appear in animal or human form.

Shepherd: Shepherd is one of the six angels of repentance. He was also guardian angel to Hermas, author of the early Christian best-seller, *Shepherd of Hermas.*
See *guardian angels.*

Sheratiel (Sharatiel): Sheratiel is the angel of Leo who assists Archangel Verchiel in looking after people born under this sign.
See *Archangels, Verchiel.*

Shimshiel: See *Shamshiel.*

Sidriel (Sabrael): According to the Third Book of Enoch, Sidriel is the Archangel in charge of the First Heaven. He is assisted by 496,000 myriads of angels. As Sabrael, he is believed to be Prince of the Tarshishim.
See *Archangels, Tarshishim.*

Simiel: Simiel is one of the angels who were demoted at the Council of Rome in 745 CE. Pope Zachary became concerned at the public interest in angels and declared a number of them could no longer be venerated. These angels, known as reprobated angels, are: Adimus, Inias, Raguel, Sabaoc, Simiel, Tubuas, and Uriel.
See individual angels, *reprobated angels.*

Sirael (Sih-rah-el) **(Sitael):** Sirael is a member of the choir of Seraphim. He is also one of the seventy-two Schemhamphoras, a group of angels who bear the various names of God found in Jewish scriptures. He is guardian angel for people born between April 1 and 4. He is interested in helping people combine idealism, thought, and practicality to start new ventures.
See *guardian angels, Schemhamphoras.*

Sizouse: In ancient Persia, Sizouse was the angel who presided over prayers and delivered them to the Throne of God.

See *Throne of God.*

Sopheriel Mehayye (Sopheriel, Sofriel, or Soperiel YHWH): In Jewish lore, Sopheriel Mehayye is one of the eight Merkabah angels and a member of the Sarim. He looks after the books of the dead and records everyone's date of death using a quill of fire.

See *Merkabah, Sarim.*

Sopheriel Memeth (Soperiel YWHW): In Jewish lore, Sopheriel Memeth is one of the eight Merkabah angels and a member of the Sarim. He looks after the books of the living and uses a quill of fire to record the names of everyone who is alive.

See *Merkabah, Sarim.*

Sophia (Pistis Sophia): "Wisdom." Sophia is one of the most important aeons. Some people consider Sophia to be the greatest of all angels, believing that she gave birth to all the other angels. According to Gnostic tradition, Sophia sent the serpent to tempt Eve. Sophia is always shown as a female angel wearing crimson robes and sitting on a throne.

See *aeons.*

Soqed Hozi (So-theth Ho-zee) **(Soqedhozi YHWH):** In Jewish lore, Soqed Hozi is one of the eight Merkabah angels, a member of the choir of Thrones, and a Sarim angel-prince. He looks after the scale on which all human souls are weighed, and he constantly grieves at the amount of human wickedness.

See *Merkabah, Sarim, Thrones.*

Soul, Angels of the: According to Jewish legend, five angels are responsible for leading the souls of people to receive the judgment of God. They are: Araqiel, Aziel, Rumael, Samael, and Uriel.

See *Aziel, Samael, Uriel.*

Spenta Armaiti: In Zoroastrianism, Spenta Armaiti is the angel of devotion. She is considered a female angel and is an Amesha Spenta (Archangel). She is believed to have appeared to Zoroaster when he was starting his new religion. She is in charge of the earth and looks after people who care for the planet. Her main interests are peace, harmony, goodness, devotion, and the truth. Spenta Armaiti can be invoked when it is important to determine the truth of a matter.

See *Amesha Spentas, Archangels, Zoroastrianism.*

Spenta Mainyu: In Zoroastrianism, Spenta Mainyu is the Holy Spirit created by Ahura Mazda, the Wise Lord, to fight against Angra Mainyu, the devil. Spenta Mainyu is considered to be an aspect of Ahura Mazda, and followers of Zoroastrianism believe he provides them with love and protection.

See *Ahura Mazda, Angra Mainyu, devil, Zoroastrianism.*

Splenditenes: In Manicheanism, Splenditenes supported the Heavens on his back. Another angel, Omophorus, carried the world on his shoulders. St. Augustine mentioned Splenditenes in *Contra Faustum XV*, and wrote that he had six faces and glittered with light.

See *Omophorus.*

Sraosha (Sa-rosh) **(Sirush):** "Hearkening" Sraosha is the yazata angel of divine intuition. He patiently listens to people's complaints about their experiences with evil. Sraosha also helps Mithra and Rashnu judge the souls of the dead. He also has the important task of carrying the souls of the dead into the next world. In his spare time, usually during the night, he protects the righteous by chasing demons and other evil spirits. Sraosha has a chariot and four fast white horses to enable him to travel from his home on Mount Haraiti.

See *demon, Mithra, Rashnu, yazata,* Zoroastrianism.

Sstiel YHWH (Sis-tee-yel Yah-way): Sstiel YHWH is one of the eight most important Merkabah angels. In the Third Book of Enoch, even the mighty Metatron has to dismount when he comes across Sstiel YHWH on the crystal roads.

See *Merkabah, Metatron.*

Steiner, Rudolf: Rudolf Steiner (1861–1925), the founder of Anthroposophy, was born in Kraljevec, Croatia. At the age of forty, he began writing and lecturing on esoteric subjects. Eleven years later, in 1912, he established the Anthroposophical Society. Rudolf Steiner wrote many books on spiritual topics and had a great interest in angels, especially Archangel Michael. In fact, he considered himself to be in the service of this great Archangel. Rudolf Steiner believed seven Archangels took turns exerting their special influence on humanity, and it was Michael who looked after the world for most of Steiner's life:

Michael: 600–200 BCE
Oriphiel: 200 BCE–150 CE
Anael: 150–500 CE
Zachariel: 500–850 CE
Raphael: 850–1190 CE
Samael: 1190–1510 CE
Gabriel: 1510–1879 CE
Michael: 1879 CE–present

Rudolf Steiner also developed his own hierarchy of angels. He believed every person has his or her own personal guardian angel but could not receive the benefit of this until opening his or her soul to the ineffable love of the guardian angel.

See *Anthroposophy, Archangels, guardian angels, hierarchy of angels,* individual angels.

Sukallin: The ancient Sumerians and Babylonians had angel-like messengers and servants for their god, Marduk. These messengers were called sukallin. Sukallin are probably the immediate predecessors of the Zoroastrian angels. Nabo was a sukallin before being considered a god. Today, he is once again considered an angel.

See *Nabo*.

Suriel: Suriel is an Archangel who taught Moses. Because of the huge influence he had on the life of Moses, God allowed him to come down to earth to retrieve Moses' soul. Suriel, Gabriel, Michael, Raphael, and Saraqael are all called great Archangels in the First Book of Enoch. Suriel is also one of the ruling angels of the zodiac and is responsible for the sign of Taurus.

See *Archangels*, individual angels, *zodiac (angels of the)*.

Swedenborg, Emmanuel: Emmanuel Swedenborg (1688–1772) was a Swedish scientist and mystic who wrote many books on algebra, astronomy, chemistry, and navigation. However, after the age of fifty, he dedicated himself to communicating with angels and wrote many books based on what they told him. His most important book is *Heaven and Hell*, which discusses angels, demons, God, Heaven, and Hell. Swedenborg believed people could see angels using their spiritual eyes, rather than their physical eyes. He also believed that all angels had originally lived on earth as men and women. After his death, his followers founded the Church of the New Religion based on his teachings. The Swedenborgian Foundation continues to this day, keeping his books in print.

See *demon*.

Tadhiel: "Righteousness of God." According to Jewish legend, Tadhiel was the angel God sent to prevent Abraham from sacrificing his son, Isaac. Metatron and Zadkiel have also been credited with this task. The Bible account does not mention the angel by name: "And the angel of the Lord called upon him out of Heaven, and said, Abraham, Abraham: and he said, Here am I. And he said, Lay not thine hand upon the lad, neither do thou any thing unto him: for now I know that thou fearest God, seeing thou hast not withheld thy son, thine only son from me" (Genesis 22:11–12).

See *Metatron, Zadkiel.*

Taftafiah: Taftafiah is an angel who is mentioned in fourth-century Jewish literature. His name is constructed from the first two letters of three verses (69, 70, and 76) of Psalm 119.

Tagas: Tagas is head of both the Sarim and the parasim. He is so important that even the four great Archangels (Raphael, Michael, Gabriel, and Uriel) bow down before him. In the Third Book of

Enoch, he is described as being in charge of the angelic choirs that constantly sing God's praises.

See *Archangels*, individual angels, *parasim*, *Sarim*.

Tagriel: Tagriel is said to be one of the chief guards in the Second or Seventh Heaven. He is also one of the twenty-eight angels who govern the mansions of the moon. Tagriel is responsible for Alpharg, the twenty-sixth mansion. In this role, he destroys prisons and other buildings and ensures the health of prisoners.

See *mansions of the moon*.

Tahariel: Tahariel is the angel of chastity and purification. He encourages cleanliness of mind and body. Tahariel is the angel to call on when you need a respite from everyday relationships and are seeking a greater association with the Divine. This time can be short or long, but it will purify your body, mind, heart, and soul.

Taliahad: Taliahad is the angel who helps Archangel Gabriel look after the element of water.

See *Archangels*, *Gabriel*.

Tarot, Angels of the: Three angels are depicted in the major arcana cards of the Tarot deck. Actually, there are four, if you include Lucifer, who is depicted on the Devil card. There is some disagreement about the identity of the angels on the other cards. Most people feel that Raphael is depicted on the Lovers card, Michael on the Temperance card, and Gabriel on the Judgement card.

In addition to this, angels and Archangels have been ascribed to each of the Tarot trumps:

0 The Fool—Archangel: Raphael Ruachel (Raphael of Air); Angel: Chassan.

1 The Magician—Archangel: Raphael Kokabiel (Raphael of Mercury); Angel: Tiriel.

2 The High Priestess—Archangel: Gabriel Levannael (Gabriel of the Moon); Angel: Shelachel.

3 The Empress—Archangel: Anael; Angel: Hagiel.

4 The Emperor—Archangel: Malkhidael; Angel: Sharahiel.

5 The Hierophant—Archangel: Asmodel; Angel: Eraziel.

6 The Lovers—Archangel: Ambriel; Angel: Serayel.

7 The Chariot—Archangel: Muriel; Angel: Pakhiel.

8 Strength—Archangel: Verchiel; Angel: Sheratiel.

9 The Hermit—Archangel: Hamaliel; Angel: Shelathiel.

10 Wheel of Fortune—Archangel: Sachiel; Angel: Jophiel.

11 Justice—Archangel: Zuriel; Angel: Chadaqiel.

12 The Hanged Man—Archangel: Gabriel Maimel (Gabriel of Water); Angel: Taliahad.

13 Death—Archangel: Barchiel; Angel: Sayitziel.

14 Temperance—Archangel: Adnachiel; Angel: Saritaiel.

15 The Devil—Archangel: Anael; Angel: Samaqiel.

16 The Tower—Archangel: Zamael; Angel: Graphiel.

17 The Star—Archangel: Cambiel; Angel: Tzakmaqiel.

18 The Moon—Archangel: Amnitziel; Angel: Vakhabiel.

19 The Sun—Archangel: Michael Shemeshel (Michael of the Sun); Angel: Nakhiel.

20 Judgement—Archangels: Michael Ashel, Metatron, and Sandalphon; Angels: Ariel and Nuriel.

21 The World—Archangels: Cassiel and Uriel; Angels: Agiel and Phorlach.

See individual angels, *Lucifer.*

Tarshish: Tarshish is a prince of the choir of Virtues and one of the rulers of the Malakhim.

See *Malakhim, Tarshishim, Virtues.*

Tarshishim: The tarshishim is a choir of angels in the Hebrew tradition. It is the equivalent of the choir of Virtues. Tarshish is usually considered their leader, though Sidriel and Anael are also sometimes mentioned.

See *Anael, Sidriel, Tarshish, Virtues.*

Teiazel: Teiazel is the angel who looks after writers, artists, sculptors, and musicians. These people can invoke him whenever they need help in their creative activities.

Teletiel: Teletiel is one of the ruling angels of the zodiac, responsible for the sign of Aries.

See *zodiac (angels of the)*.

Temeluch (Temeluchus or Temlakos): Temeluch is responsible for pregnancy, and he traditionally assists Gabriel in instructing the unborn child before it is born. He also keeps a watchful eye over newly born babies. Temeluch is a guardian angel and a childbed angel. In the Jewish tradition, there are said to be seventy childbed angels who protect mothers during childbirth and protect newborn babies from evil spirits.

However, according to the Apocalypse of Paul, Temeluch is the chief angel of torment in Hell.

See *Gabriel*.

Teoael (Tay-oh-ay-yel): Teoael is a member of the choir of Thrones. He can be invoked to help new business ventures. Traditionally, he was invoked to protect ships heading out to sea with precious cargoes.

See *Thrones*.

Terathel (Ierathel, Yeratel): Terathel is the guardian angel of people born between April 2 and 6. He is a member of the Dominions and is an angel of joy, laughter, and optimism.

See *Dominions, guardian angels*.

Teresa of Avila, Saint: St. Teresa of Avila (1515–1582) is one of the most popular saints in the Catholic Church. She entered a Carmelite convent in 1535, and, despite much hostility, founded the first convent of Carmelite Reform in 1562. In 1555, she began experiencing visions in which she heard voices. This disturbed her until St. Peter of Alcantara, her spiritual adviser, told her they were angel visitations. After that, she communicated with angels regularly, and one beautiful angel appeared to her in bodily form. He thrust a golden spear into her heart, causing a pain she described as "sweet." St. Teresa wrote many books, including an autobiography. She is best known for her books describing the progress of the human soul as it moves inexorably toward God.

Tetragrammaton: The Tetragrammaton is YHVH, the four consonants (Yod, Heh, Vau, Heh) that spell the holy, unspeakable name of God. Because it is so sacred, even today, many Jews say "Adonai" ("Lord") to avoid saying the name out loud. Early Christians pronounced it as "Jehovah," but modern-day scholars feel it should be pronounced "Yaweh," and therefore it is sometimes spelled YHWH. Many people say the individual letters, in preference to the name. In some traditions, the seventy-three most important angels have YHVH added to their names. This is known as a *tetragram*, and it entitles them to speak in the Great Law Court in Heaven. The Tetragrammaton also plays a major role in the Kabbalah.

Tezalel: Tezalel is the angel responsible for trust and fidelity in all loving relationships. He works hard to keep couples together, as long as there is a good chance of saving the relationship. Sometimes, if the couple has drifted apart, Tezalel recognizes it might be better for them to separate rather than continue in a dead relationship. You can call on Tezalel if you have any concerns about the quality of your relationship.

Theliel: Theliel is the angelic prince of love. Not surprisingly, he is associated with the planet Venus. Men should call on him if they want to attract love into their lives. Theliel will not make a specific person fall in love with you, as this might not be in the best interest of both parties. However, he will create desirable situations to help people meet each other. After that, it is up to the two people to develop a relationship, if they wish.

Throne Bearers: The throne bearers are an exclusive choir of angels in Islam. Until the Day of Judgment, only four angels belong to this group. However, this will be increased to eight on the day of Resurrection.

Throne of God: According to Jewish legend, God sits on his throne in Heaven while the court of Heaven assesses the deeds of men and women. Seven Archangels stand at the throne. Twenty-four Elders sit on thrones surrounding the throne of God. The Seraphim, Cherubim, and Thrones encircle the throne of God. When the court is in session, the angels of mercy stand on the right-hand side of God, the angels of peace stand to His left, and the angels of punishment stand in front of Him. When they are all assembled, Radueriel breaks the seals on the box that contains the record of everyone's deeds and hands the scrolls to God (3 Enoch 27:1–2).

See *Archangels, Cherubim, Elders, punishment (angels of), Radueriel, Seraphim, Thrones.*

Thrones: The Thrones are the third-highest ranking of angels in Dionysius the Areopagite's hierarchy of angels. They are sometimes called Wheels, as Ezekiel, the Old Testament prophet, saw them as fiery wheels. They are angels of justice. Their task is to advise God when he makes important decisions. According to the Testament of Adam, they stand in front of the throne of God. The princes of the choir of Thrones include: Jophiel, Orifiel, Raziel, and Zaphkiel. Artists usually depict the Thrones as fiery wheels, with four wings that are covered with penetrating eyes.

See *Dionysius the Areopagite, hierarchy of angels,* individual angels.

Thunder: In the Islamic tradition, Thunder is the angel who looks after the clouds and sends them wherever Archangel Michael decides they should go. Thunder wields a large stick that he uses to make the clouds move. Whenever we hear the sound of thunder, we are hearing the angel Thunder praising God. Thunder has an assistant named Annan.

See *Annan, Archangels, Michael*.

Tir: Tir is the yazata angel in charge of Mercury and the month of June. Tir has the body of a fish, the face of a boar, and two arms (one white and the other black). He wears a crown.

See *yazata, Zoroastrianism*.

Tiriel: Tiriel helps Raphael look after the planet Mercury. Magicians invoke him when making talismans relating to Mercury. It is likely that Tiriel was originally Tir and became Tiriel when adopted by the Hebrew pantheon of angels.

See *Raphael*.

Tomimiel: Tomimiel is one of the ruling angels of the zodiac, responsible for the sign of Gemini.

See *zodiac (angels of the)*.

Tsaphiel: Tsaphiel is one of the angels of the moon, sometimes invoked by magicians when performing rituals involving the moon.

Tubuas (Tubuael): Tubuas is one of the angels who were demoted at the Council of Rome in 745 CE. Pope Zachary became concerned at the public interest in angels and declared a number of them could no longer be venerated. These angels, known as reprobated angels, are: Adimus, Inias, Raguel, Sabaoc, Simiel, Tubuas, and Uriel.

See *individual angels, reprobated angels*.

Tzadkiel: See *Zadkiel*.

Tzakmaqiel (Tsak-mak-ee-el) (**Tzakmiqiel or Tzakamquiel**): Tzak-maqiel is the angel of Aquarius, and he helps Archangel Cambiel look after people born under this sign.

See *Archangels, Cambiel, zodiac (angels of the)*.

Tzaphiel (Tsaf-ee-el) (**Tzaphkiel or Tzaphquiel**): According to the Zohar, Tzaphiel is third of the ten Archangels and is responsible for Binah in the Tree of Life. His duties include looking after Thursdays and Saturdays.

See *Archangels*.

Umbael (Oo-ma-bel) **(Umabel):** Umbael is one of the seventy-two Schemhamphoras, a group of angels who bear the various names of God found in Jewish scriptures. He is guardian angel of people born between January 21 and 25. He encourages a sensitive and nurturing approach to problems and difficulties. Umbael enjoys helping people who are interested in astronomy and physics.

See *guardian angels, Schemhamphoras.*

Uriel (Oo-ree-el): "Fire of God." Uriel is the Archangel of prophecy. He is usually listed as one of the four main Archangels. The others are Michael, Gabriel, and Raphael. However, unlike those three, Uriel does not appear in the Scriptures, which means we know of him only through stories and legends. Uriel is sometimes considered an Angel of the Presence and has also been classified as both a Cherubim and Seraphim. He is one of the Sarim angel-princes. Uriel is also Regent of the Sun and is in charge of all natural phenomena, such as floods and earthquakes. In Jewish legend, Uriel warned Noah of the imminent flood. He is also the overseer of Hell. Uriel holds the keys to Hell and will destroy the gates to Hell on Judgment Day. Uriel can be called upon to help with creative activities.

Although Uriel was considered one of the seven great Archangels by the early Christian church, he was not mentioned by name in the Bible. Consequently, at the council in Rome in 745 CE, Uriel was demoted, along with several other angels (Adimus, Inias, Raguel, Sabaoc, Simiel, and Tubuas). They are known as the reprobated angels.

Artists usually depict Uriel holding a scroll in one hand, with an open flame burning on his other hand. This flame symbolizes his name, "Fire of God."

See *Archangels*, *Cherubim*, individual angels, *Presence (Angels of the)*, *reprobated angels*, *Sarim*, *Seraphim*.

Urpaniel: Urpaniel is an angel in Judaism who was occasionally used on protective amulets.

Ushahin: Ushahin is the yazata angel in Zoroastrianism who looks after the hours from midnight to dawn every day.
See *yazata*, *Zoroastrianism*.

Uzerin: Uzerin is the yazata angel in Zoroastrianism who looks after the hours from 3 PM until sunset every day.
See *yazata*, *Zoroastrianism*.

Uzzah: "The Lord is Strength." Uzzah, Azzah, and Azael are listed in the Third Book of Enoch as the angels who did not want Enoch to be transformed into the angel Metatron. They told God that Enoch was a descendent of people who had been drowned in the Flood for their wicked ways and that he did not deserve to become an angel. God told them they had no right to interfere and that he had chosen Enoch ahead of any angel. Uzzah, Azzah, and Azael were smart enough to accept the rebuff and bowed down before the new angelic prince, Metatron. Despite this, the angels teased

Metatron by calling him "youth," because he was the youngest angel.

See *Azael, Azzah, Metatron*.

Uzziel (Usiel): "God's Power." Uzziel is the angel of mercy. Some sources claim he is a Cherubim or chief of the order of Virtues. He provides faith and hope in our darkest moments. Uzziel is the angel to invoke when everything seems hopeless and there seems no point in carrying on. He also works hard to teach people faith, hope, love, and forgiveness. According to the apocryphal Book of the Angel Raziel, Uzziel is one of the seven angels who stand in front of the Throne of God.

See *Cherubim, Virtues, Throne of God*.

Vakhabiel (Vakabiel or Vacabiel): Vakhabiel is the angel of Pisces who helps Archangel Amnitziel look after people born under this sign.

See *Amnitziel, Archangels, zodiac (angels of the).*

Valoel (Valuel): Valoel provides peace, contentment, and understanding. When life is overly hectic or tumultuous, Valoel can provide the necessary peace of mind to handle the situation.

Vasiariah (Va-sah-ree-yah) **(Vasariah or Variariah):** Vasiariah belongs to the Dominions and looks after justice, lawyers, judges, and courts of law. He can be invoked in any matters concerning justice, honesty, and fairness. Vasariah is also one of the seventy-two Schemhamphoras, a group of angels who bear the various names of God found in Jewish scriptures. Vasiariah is guardian angel of people born between August 29 and September 2.

See *Dominions, guardian angels, Schemhamphoras.*

Vayu: Vayu is a yazata angel in Zoroastrianism. He is responsible for winds and the air.

See *yazata, Zoroastrianism.*

Vehael (Vay-hay-el) **(Vahuel or Vehuel):** Vehael is a member of the Principalities and one of the seventy-two Schemhamphoras, a group of angels who bear the various names of God found in Jewish scriptures. He is guardian angel for people born between November 23 and 27. Vehael promotes creativity and pleasure.

See *guardian angels, Principalities, Schemhamphoras.*

Vehujah (Vay-hoo-ee-yah) **(Vehuiah):** In the Kabbalah, Vehujah is one of the eight Seraphim. He is also one of the seventy-two Schemhamphoras, a group of angels who bear the various names of God found in Jewish scriptures. Vehujah is guardian angel for people born between March 21 and 25. He enjoys helping people gain confidence and self-esteem.

See *guardian angels, Schemhamphoras, Seraphim.*

Verchiel (Verkhiel, Verkiel, or Varchiel): Verchiel is one of the regents of the choir of Powers. Verchiel is the Archangel responsible for the sign of Leo and the month of July. According to some sources, Verchiel is also a prince in the choir of Virtues. He provides love, affection, and friendship. You should call on Verchiel when you are experiencing difficulties with family or good friends.

See *Archangels, Powers, Virtues, zodiac (angels of the).*

Verethraghna: Verethraghna is the yazata of success and victory. He is the strongest and fastest Zoroastrian angel. He works for honesty and kindness and punishes evil-doers. He takes on a wide range of forms to carry out his work. These include: a strong wind, a bull with gold horns, a powerful white horse, a camel, a bear, a bird, a bull, a young man, and a warrior wielding a sword.

See *yazata, Zoroastrianism.*

Vevaliah (Vay-vah-lee-ah) **(Veualiah or Veuliah):** Vevaliah is a member of the choir of Virtues and is also one of the seventy-two Schemhamphoras, a group of angels who bear the various names of God found in Jewish scriptures. Vevaliah is guardian angel for people born between October 24 and 28. As a Virtue, Vevaliah is involved in high-level activities, but he also enjoys encouraging and motivating people in their everyday lives.

See *guardian angels, Schemhamphoras, Virtues.*

Victoricus (Victorius or Victor): Victoricus was guardian angel to St. Patrick (c.385–461), the patron saint of Ireland. He appeared to St. Patrick on a weekly basis to offer advice and friendship. Patrick had been kidnapped at the age of sixteen and was taken from Roman Britain to Ireland, where he became a slave looking after pigs. An angelic voice helped him escape to France. It was Victoricus who asked St. Patrick to return to Ireland to convert the people there to Christianity.

See *guardian angels.*

Virgin Mary: In the Roman Catholic Church, the Virgin Mary is considered Queen of the Angels.

See *Queen of Angels.*

Virgin of Light: The Manichaeans believed in a great angel called the Virgin of Light, who lived in the moon. In the Gnostic *Pistis Sophia*, the Virgin of Light is the judge of souls, a task normally carried out by Sophia. One of her tasks is to decide which soul is to be placed into each new body at conception. Consequently, the Virgin of Light placed the soul of Elijah into the body of the baby who grew up to become John the Baptist.

See *Sophia.*

Virtues: The Virtues are the fifth-highest rank of angels in the hierarchy of angels devised by Dionysius the Areopagite. They are in charge of all natural laws to keep the universe working as it should. Because of this, in the Hebrew tradition, they are also responsible for miracles that go against these laws. As the apostles watched Christ ascend into Heaven, they were joined by two men "in white apparel" (Acts 1:10). These are traditionally believed to be two members of the choir of Virtues. Archangel Michael is Prince Regent of the choir of Virtues. The other princes include Barbiel, Gabriel, Peliel, Raphael, and Uzziel. At one time, Satan was also a member of this order. Artists usually depict the Virtues as bishops carrying either a lily or a red rose (to symbolize the passion of Christ). They have a golden belt around their waists.

See *Archangels*, *Dionysius the Areopagite*, individual angels, *Satan*.

Vohu Manah: Vohu Manah is one of the leading Amesha Spentas (Archangels) in Zoroastrianism. He is the angel of self-worth, love, and divine wisdom. Vohu Manah guided Zoroaster's soul to the Throne of God. Vohu Manah welcomes the souls of good people as they enter Heaven. Members of the Zoroastrian religion are told to "bring down Vohu Manah in your lives on Earth." They do this by loving their marriage partners as well as their neighbors. Vohu Manah is also the protector of all animals and the guardian angel of cattle.

See *Amesha Spentas*, *Throne of God*, *Zoroaster*, *Zoroastrianism*.

Vretil: See *Radueriel*.

War in Heaven: The war in Heaven began when Satan refused God's order to bow down to Adam. Satan gathered an army of angels to fight God's forces, which were led by Archangel Michael. In the Middle Ages, people believed Satan's forces numbered 133,306,668—a huge army by any standards. The Bible reads: "And there was war in Heaven: Michael and his angels fought against the dragon; and the dragon fought and his angels, and prevailed not; neither was their place found any more in Heaven. And the great dragon was cast out, that old serpent, called the devil, and Satan, which deceiveth the whole world: he was cast out into the earth, and his angels were cast out with him" (Revelation 12:7–9).

Satan and his army became fallen angels. They now live in Hell, where they still scheme and plot against God, even though they know the task is impossible. Satan and his army will be defeated again at the end of time.

See *Archangels, fallen angels, Michael, Satan.*

Watchers: Originally, the watchers were an important choir of angels. The best-known watchers are the Grigori, the fallen angels who are part of Jewish legend. They came down to earth to teach mankind knowledge that God thought would be useful to them. Unfortunately, some of them fell in love with human women, and the children who were born as a result were the giants Nephilim. Shemhazai was the leader of the Grigori. However, there are two other watchers who, according to the Third Book of Enoch, are called the Irin. They are twin angels who discuss and debate every issue that comes before the throne of God. These watchers are mentioned in Daniel 4:17.

See *fallen angels*, *Grigori*, *Irin (the)*, *Nephilim*, *Shemhazai*.

Water, Angel of: See *Taliahad*.

Week, Angels of the: Angels are responsible for the different days of the week. Magicians invoke these angels on their respective days to help them in their endeavors. Various names have been suggested for the different names of the week, but the best-known selection is the one published in *The Magus* (1801) by Francis Barrett:

Sunday: Michael
Monday: Gabriel
Tuesday: Camael (Chamuel)
Wednesday: Raphael
Thursday: Sachiel
Friday: Anael
Saturday: Cassiel

Peter de Abano (c.1250–c.1316), the Italian philosopher, listed his selection in his book *Heptameron* (Magical Elements) on angels:

Sunday: Michael
Monday: Gabriel
Tuesday: Samael

Wednesday: Raphael
Thursday: Sachiel
Friday: Anael
Saturday: Cassiel

The *Liber Juratus*, also known as *The Sworn Book of Honorius*, was a famous thirteenth-century grimoire that influenced many generations of magicians, including Dr. John Dee. It listed 47 angels for Sunday, 56 for Monday, 52 for Tuesday, 45 for Wednesday, 37 for Thursday, 47 for Friday, and 50 for Saturday.

See *day (angels of the)*, *Dee (Dr. John)*, individual angels, *planetary angels*.

Wheels: This is another name for the choir of Thrones.
See *Thrones*.

Wormwood: Wormwood is a bitter-tasting plant, making it an unlikely name for an angel. Although it is called a star in the Bible (Revelation 8:11), Wormwood is generally considered an angel: "And the third angel sounded, and there fell a great star from Heaven, burning as it were a lamp, and it fell upon the third part of the rivers, and upon the fountains of waters; And the name of the star is called Wormwood: and the third part of the waters became wormwood; and many men died of the waters, because they were made bitter" (Revelation 8:10–11). C. S. Lewis (1898–1963) made Wormwood a junior devil in his novel *The Screwtape Letters*.

Xaphan (Zephon): Xaphan was one of Satan's soldiers in the war in Heaven. He suggested to Satan that they set fire to Heaven, but they were defeated before their plan could be carried out. Xaphan became one of the fallen angels and spends his time fanning the flames in the furnaces of Hell.

See *fallen angels, Satan, war in Heaven.*

Xathanael (Nathanel or Nathaniel): According to one version of The Gospel of Bartholomew, Xathanael was the sixth angel created by God. Not surprisingly, the Catholic Church, which believes all angels were created simultaneously, does not accept this idea.

See *Nathanel.*

Yahriel: Yahriel is one of the angels of the moon and is sometimes invoked by magicians when performing rituals involving the moon.

Yazata (Yazad): "Adorable Ones." The yazatas are Zoroastrian angels who serve under the Amesha Spentas and work to help and protect humankind. The head of the yazatas is Mithra, whose main task is to assist Ahura Mazda, the God in Zoroastrianism. Some of the better known yazata include: Aban, Ahurani, Airyaman, Akhshti, Arshtat, Ashi Vanghuhi, Asman, Atar, Chista, Daena, Erethe, Havani, Hvare-Khshaeta, Maonghah, Meher, Mithra, Nairyosangha, Parendi, Raman, Rapithwin, Rasanstat, Rashnu, Rata, Sraosha, Ushahin, Uzerin, Vayu, and Zamyat.

See *Ahura Mazda, Amesha Spentas,* individual angels, *Mithra, Zoroastrianism.*

Yazidi: The Yazidi are followers of a Kurdish religious sect that predates Christianity. There are about 500,000 Yazidis worldwide in Iraq, Iran, Armenia, Georgia, Syria, Turkey, and Russia. They believe in a creator god who has seven angels to help him look after the world. The head angel is Melek Ta'us, usually known as the Peacock Angel. In Yazidi teaching, God created the Peacock Angel first, followed by the other six angels. God asked the angels to bring him dust from the earth. God blew his breath into this dust and created Adam, the first man. Although some people claim the Peacock Angel is a fallen angel, the Yazidis consider him a major force for good, and God trusts him to look after the earth. The Yazidis do not believe in a devil or any other spiritual adversary fighting against God. There are eight Archangels in the Yazidi pantheon: Melek Ta'us (Peacock Angel), Kadir-Rahman, Sheikh Bakra, Sheikh Ism, Sij-ed-din, Nasr-ed-din, Fakr-ed-din, and Shams-ed-din.

See *fallen angels, Melek Ta'us*.

Yefifiyyah (Yefefiah or Yepipyah): Yefifiyyah is an Angel of the Presence and a member of the Sarim. Jewish legend says he taught the Kabbalah to Moses.

See *Presence (Angels of the), Sarim*.

Yehudiah (Yay-hoo-dee-yah) **(Yehudiam):** Yehudiah is the angel of bereavement and can be called upon for comfort when a loved one dies. He also helps carry the souls of the dead up to Heaven. Because of this, he is considered an angel of death in Judaism. He is one of God's chief messengers and is the guardian angel of people born between September 3 and 7.

See *death (angel of), guardian angels*.

Yetzer Hara (Yetzer Ra): In the Jewish tradition, Yetzer Hara symbolizes the dark, or evil, side of everyone's nature. He is often thought to be the angel of death and/or Satan.

See *death (angel of), Satan*.

YHVH: The four consonants YHVH are known as the Tetragrammaton. They are sometimes expressed as YHWH, to match the popular "Yaweh" pronunciation. They spell God's true name in Hebrew. God's true name was considered too sacred to be spoken out loud, and people referred to Adonai, or Lord, instead. In some traditions, the seventy-three most important Archangels have these four letters added to their names. Metatron is known as the Lesser YHVH.

See *Archangels, Tetragrammaton.*

Yophiel (Iofiel or Yofiel): Yophiel is the Jewish angel of beauty. In Jewish tradition, Yophiel, Metatron, and Yefifiyyah placed Moses on his couch immediately before he died. In the Zohar, Yophiel is considered one of the leading angels, with fifty-three legions of lesser angels attending him.

See *Jophiel, Metatron, Yefifiyyah.*

Za'amiel: According to the Third Book of Enoch, Za'amiel is one of the Rulers of the Earth and is responsible for vehemence.
See *Rulers of the Earth.*

Za'aphiel (Za'afiel): , Za'aphiel is one of the Rulers of the Earth, according to the Third Book of Enoch. He is responsible for hurricanes and storms. Apparently, God sometimes uses Za'aphiel to deal with evildoers.
See *Rulers of the Earth.*

Zabkiel: See *Zaphkiel.*

Zachariel: Zachariel has been listed among the Archangels, Dominions, and Powers. He can be invoked to help people improve their memory. Rudolf Steiner considered him one of the seven great Archangels. It is possible that he helps Archangel Raphael rule over the second of the seven Heavens.
See *Archangels, Dominions, Heavens, Powers, Raphael, Steiner (Rudolf).*

Zadkiel (Zachiel or Tzadkiel): "Righteousness of God." Zadkiel is the ruler of Jupiter, regent of Sagittarius, ruler of the Fifth Heaven, a member of the Sarim, and is believed to be Chief of the Choir of Dominions. Zadkiel is also the Angel of Divine Justice and a planetary angel. Dionysius the Areopagite included Zadkiel in his list of seven Archangels. In the Fifth Heaven, Zadkiel is attended by 496,000 myriads of angels. Because of his association with Jupiter, Zadkiel provides abundance, benevolence, mercy, forgiveness, tolerance, compassion, prosperity, happiness, and good fortune. According to Jewish legend, it was Zadkiel who prevented Abraham from sacrificing his son Isaac. (However, another Jewish legend says Tadhiel performed this task.) You should call on Zadkiel for help whenever you experience financial or legal problems. It is possible that Zadkiel and Sachiel are two names for the same angel. As Tzadkiel, his name is sometimes found on amulets worn by pregnant women who believe he will help them give birth to a healthy baby.

See *Archangels, Dionysius the Areopagite, Dominions, planetary angels, Sachiel, Sarim, Tadhiel.*

Zagzagel: "God's Righteousness." In Hebrew lore, Zagzagel is the angel of the burning bush who gave advice to Moses (Exodus 3:2). Zagzagel advised and taught Moses, and he helped Michael and Gabriel prepare Moses' grave and escort his soul to Heaven. Zagzagel is believed to be an Angel of the Presence, ruler of the Fourth Heaven, and a member of the Sarim. Although he looks after the Fourth Heaven, Zagzagel lives close to God in the Seventh Heaven. In his spare time, he also teaches other angels. He speaks seventy languages. You can call on Zagzagel whenever you need knowledge or wisdom.

See *Gabriel, Michael, Presence (Angels of the).*

Zakun (Zakum): Zakun is a powerful angel who, with Lahash, led 184 myriads of angels to seize the prayers of the Jews who were praying that Moses be allowed to reach the Promised Land.

Lahash was severely punished for this transgression, but Zakun's fate is not known.

See *Lahash.*

Zamael: "The Severity of God." Zamael is the Archangel of the planet Mars and the angel who looks after Tuesday. There has been considerable confusion between three Archangels: Khamael, Samael, and Zamael. It is possible they are all the same angel.

See *Archangels, Khamael, Samael.*

Zamyat: Zamyat is the female yazata angel in Zoroastrianism who rules over the earth.

See *yazata, Zoroastrianism.*

Zaphiel: Zaphiel is mentioned in the Third Book of Enoch. He has been called a Cherubim and ruler of the planet Saturn. One legend says he taught Noah before Noah started building the ark.

See *Cherubim.*

Zaphkiel: Zaphkiel is a prince of the choir of Thrones. He is one of the planetary angels who look after the planet Saturn. It is possible that Zaphkiel is another name for Cassiel.

See *Cassiel, planetary angels, Thrones.*

Zarall: Zarall and Jael were two Cherubim who protected the Ark of the Covenant. Depictions of them were carved into the mercy seat of the Ark.

See *Ark of the Covenant, Cherubim, Jael.*

Zebul: Zebul is one of the two rulers of the Sixth Heaven. He rules the nighttime hours, and Sabath rules during the daytime.

See *Heavens, Sabath.*

Zebuleon: According to the Book of Esdras, Zebuleon is one of the nine angels who will govern the world after the Day of Judgment.

The others are: Aker, Arphugitonos, Beburos, Gabriel, Gabuthelon, Michael, Raphael, and Uriel.

See individual angels.

Zedekiel: See *Zadkiel*.

Zehanpuryu YHWH: In Jewish legend, Zehanpuryu YHWH is one of the gatekeepers to the Seventh Heaven. This makes him one of the most important angels in Heaven.

See *Heavens*.

Zequiel: Zequiel is an unusual angel who came to help Eugene Torralva, a Spanish doctor who lived in Rome in the early sixteenth century. Zequiel, who looked like a young man with blonde hair and a black over-robe, taught Torralva the healing powers of several plants, which the doctor was able to use with his patients. However, Zequiel's specialty was predicting the future, and on at least two occasions he transported Torralva through the air on a knotted stick to see an actual event unfold. Not surprisingly, word of this got out and Torralva was arrested by the Inquisition in 1528. After being tortured, Torralva admitted that Zequiel was an evil spirit and that he would have no more dealings with him.

Zi'iel: According to the Third Book of Enoch, Zi'iel is one of the Rulers of the Earth and is responsible for ground tremors and commotion.

See *Rulers of the Earth*.

Ziqiel: According to the Third Book of Enoch, Ziqiel is one of the Rulers of the Earth and is responsible for comets.

See *Rulers of the Earth*.

Zodiac, Angels of the: Angels have been associated with the twelve signs of the zodiac for thousands of years. It is a logical association, as angels, stars, and planets are all associated with the celestial realms. According to Jewish tradition, Masleh is the angel in charge of the zodiac. Abbot Johannes Trithemius included the traditional associations of angels with the astrological signs in *The Book of Secret Things* (c.1500):

Aries: Malahidael or Machidiel
Taurus: Asmodel
Gemini: Ambriel
Cancer: Muriel
Leo: Verchiel
Virgo: Hamaliel
Libra: Zuriel or Uriel
Scorpio: Barbiel
Sagittarius: Advachiel or Adnachiel
Capricorn: Hanael (See Anael)
Aquarius: Cambiel or Gabriel
Pisces: Barchiel

Medieval magicians called on the angels of the zodiac for many purposes, and many different angels were related to the twelve signs. In his *Three Books of Occult Philosophy*, Cornelius Agrippa mentioned twelve other angels who are frequently associated with the signs of the zodiac (p. 553). However, he made two mistakes in his list (the angels for Cancer and Libra). Dr. Thomas Rudd (1583–1656) recorded a more accurate list that is included in *Summoning the Solomonic Archangels & Demon Princes* by Stephen Skinner and David Rankine:

Aries: Teletiel
Taurus: Suriel
Gemini: Tomimiel
Cancer: Sataniel
Leo: Ariel
Virgo: Botuliel
Libra: Masniel
Scorpio: Acrabiel

Sagittarius: Chosetiel
Capricorn: Godiel
Aquarius: Deliel
Pisces: Dagymiel

See individual angels.

Zoroaster: (c. 628–c. 551 BCE) Zoroaster was an Iranian prophet, religious reformer, and founder of Zoroastrianism. According to the Zend Avesta, the sacred book of Zoroastrianism, Zoroaster saw Ahura Mazda in a vision. Ahura Mazda told him to teach others his philosophy of good thoughts, words, and deeds. Zoroaster's teaching has had a huge effect, not only on the Persian civilization, but also on Judaism, Christianity, and Islam.

See *Ahura Mazda, Zoroastrianism.*

Zoroastrianism: Zoroastrianism is the religion founded by the Persian prophet Zoroaster in the sixth century BCE. Ahura Mazda is the deity in this religion, and he is credited with creating Heaven and earth. His chief assistants are the six or seven Amesha Spentas, the Holy Immortals, who are similar to Archangels. They constantly fight Angra Mainyu (the devil) and his supporters. Followers of Zoroastrianism believe that good will ultimately triumph over evil.

See *Ahura Mazda, Amesha Spentas, Angra Mainyu, Archangels, devil, Zoroaster, Zoroastrian angels.*

Zoroastrian Angels: In Zoroastrianism, there are six Archangels, known as Amesha Spentas, who serve Ahura Mazda (God). Ahura Mazda and his six Amesha Spentas symbolize seven moral precepts and keep watch over different aspects of Ahura Mazda's creation:

Ahura Mazda: the Holy Spirit, mankind
Vohu Manah: wisdom, cattle
Asha Vahishta: truth, fire

Armaita: devotion, earth

Khshathra Vairya: desirable dominion, sky

Haurvatat: wholeness, water

Ameretat: immortality, plants

Guardian angels are called fravashis in Zoroastrianism. Yazata are the rank and file angels in Zoroastrianism. Anahita, the angel of fertility, is an example of a yazata.

See *Ahura Mazda, Amesha Spentas, Archangels, fravashis, guardian angels*, individual angels, *yazata, Zoroastrianism*.

Zuriel: "My Rock is God." Zuriel is the Prince Regent of the choir of Principalities. He is also Archangel of the sign of Libra and ruler of September. Zuriel can be invoked to create harmony and accord. Zuriel is also the angel of childbirth, and he is sometimes summoned to help ease the pain of childbirth. In the past, pregnant women wore amulets with his name inscribed on them to provide protection during childbirth.

See *Archangels, Principalities, zodiac (angels of the)*.

Appendix

Guardian Angel Invocation

The word *invocation* is derived from the Latin *advoco*, which means, "summon." An invocation is generally performed to summon a deity, angel, or spiritual power. This appendix includes four invocations that many people have found useful in making contact with their guardian angels.

You will need both time and space to perform these invocations. Whenever possible, I prefer to do work of this sort outdoors, but naturally both privacy and the weather sometimes force me indoors. If you are performing an invocation indoors, make sure you will not be interrupted for about half an hour. I temporarily disconnect the phone to ensure there will be no interruptions. I prefer to do any magical work when I'm alone in the house, too. If this is not possible, tell the other occupants that you don't want to be disturbed for a while, to make sure they won't accidentally walk into your room in the middle of the invocation.

You will need to create a sacred space in which to perform your invocation. Start by creating a "magic circle" six to eight feet in diameter. I have a circular rug that I use when performing a ritual indoors. Alternatively, you can mark out a circle using cord or rope. Outdoors, I sometimes use stones to indicate a circle. Often, I simply imagine the circle I'm working in.

If possible, enjoy a leisurely bath before putting on clean, loose-fitting clothes. This effectively separates the invocation from your normal, everyday activities. I enjoy thinking about the invocation while washing myself and relaxing in the bath. This builds up a sense of anticipation and gives me time to think about what I hope to gain from the invocation.

Invocation One

Step into your magic circle and stand in its center. Face east, close your eyes, and visualize Archangel Raphael standing in front of you. You may visualize him as a large angel with huge wings. You might "see" him as a traveler, with a staff and a fish. You might sense him as energy, rather than a figure. It makes no difference how you visualize Raphael; what you see or sense will be right for you. When you feel Raphael is in front of you, speak to him. I prefer to speak out loud, but depending on the circumstances, you might like to talk to him in your mind. You might say something along these lines: "Thank you, Archangel Raphael, for your support and protection. I'm grateful to you for being here for me and for your guidance and healing. Thank you."

With your eyes still closed, turn to face south, and visualize Archangel Michael. I visualize him as a tall man wearing a suit of armor, with one foot resting on a dragon. This picture is a composite of different paintings I've seen of Archangel Michael over the years; naturally, you can visualize Michael in any way you wish. Again, once you sense his presence, speak to him. You might say: "Thank you, Archangel Michael, for your support and protection. Thank you for giving me strength and courage when I need it. I am very grateful for your help. Thank you."

Turn to face west. Visualize Archangel Gabriel as clearly as you can. Whatever comes into your mind is the right image for you. Speak to Gabriel: "Thank you, Archangel Gabriel, for your gentleness and devotion. Thank you for being God's messenger and for all your help and support. I am very grateful. Thank you."

Turn to face north. This time visualize Archangel Uriel before you. When you have an image in mind, speak to him: "Archangel Uriel, I'm grateful for all your help and support. Thank you for giving me fresh ideas and insights. Thank you for forcing me to make changes when I'm reluctant to make them myself. Thank you."

Turn to face Archangel Raphael again. You are now in the middle of a circle, totally surrounded by the four great Archangels. You are protected and safe. Now you can ask for anything you wish. In this particular invocation, you want to contact your personal guardian angel.

Think of your need, or desire, to make contact, and then ask your guardian angel to make himself known to you. You can ask directly, or ask the universal life force (God, Mother, Father, Allah, etc.) to intervene for you. You might say: "Thank you, [name of your guardian angel], for guiding, helping, and supporting me throughout my life. I may not have thanked you before, but I'm very grateful for everything you've done for me. Please make yourself known to me, as I wish to establish a much deeper connection with you. This will help me grow as a person, not only spiritually, but mentally, physically, and emotionally as well. Thank you once again."

Remain silent for about sixty seconds. You may find you hear almost instantly from your guardian angel. This communication will come through thoughts and insights that appear in your mind. Carry on a conversation with your guardian angel for as long as you wish. There is no need to be concerned if you don't hear from your guardian angel immediately. This invocation will have established a closer, more personal relationship with your guardian angel, and you will hear from him when the time is right.

No matter what the response is, thank your guardian angel once again. Visualize Archangel Raphael again, and thank him for his help and protection. Say goodbye, and then repeat this with Archangels Michael, Gabriel, and Uriel.

When you feel ready, open your eyes and take a few seconds to familiarize yourself with your surroundings before leaving the magic circle. Have something to eat and drink before carrying on with your day.

Once you have made a connection with your guardian angel, you will not need to perform this ritual again, as he will come to you whenever you need him. However, many people enjoy the ritual so much that they perform it regularly. It brings them into contact with the four great Archangels as well as their guardian angel.

Invocation Two

Place a table and chair in the center of your magic circle. If you wish, you can start this invocation by visualizing the four Archangels surrounding you. I like to do this not only because it's an opportunity for angelic contact, but also because of the feeling of protection the Archangels provide. However, including the Archangels is not essential.

Sit down on the chair and write a letter to your guardian angel. No one will see this letter, except for your guardian angel, so you can write anything you wish. You might thank your guardian angel for his help and support in the past. You might express your desire to contact him, and list the reasons why you want to do this. You might express your frustration at not being able to contact him in the past. Your letter must be candid, open, and honest.

Take your time in writing your letter, but do not be concerned if you accidentally miss anything you wanted to mention. You can write another letter later or discuss it in person once you've made contact.

When you have finished, sign the letter and seal it in an envelope. Place the envelope on the palm of your right hand, and rest the back of this hand on the palm of your left hand. Hold the envelope in position with your left thumb.

Close your eyes and ask your guardian angel to come to you. Allow about sixty seconds to give your guardian angel time to put thoughts into your mind. As in the previous invocation, you might make immediate contact. However, it may also take a few days. Naturally, you can enjoy a conversation with your guardian angel if contact is made. Once you have finished the conversation, or you have allowed sufficient time for contact to be made, thank your guardian angel.

When you feel ready, open your eyes. If you surrounded yourself with the Archangels, thank them for their help. Leave the magic circle.

This invocation is not quite over—you still have the letter you wrote to your guardian angel, which needs to be sent out into the universe. You do this by burning it and watching the smoke as it ascends toward Heaven. You may have to move into another room to find a safe place to burn it. As the envelope burns, visualize your message being sent to your guardian angel. Once the envelope and contents have burned away, thank your guardian angel for his help and carry on with your day.

Invocation Three

Sit in a comfortable chair with your feet flat on the ground and your hands resting in your lap. Close your eyes and take three slow, deep breaths. Each time you inhale, think, "relaxation in." When you exhale, think, "tension and stress out." Continue taking slow, deep breaths and consciously relax all of the muscles in your body, starting with your toes and finishing at the top of your head. After doing this, mentally scan your body to make sure you are totally relaxed. Focus on any areas that are still tense and allow them to completely relax.

When you are totally relaxed, focus on your breathing again. Imagine that you're breathing in divine energy each time you inhale. As you breathe out, imagine that each exhalation is creating an invisible bubble of air around you. Visualize this bubble of air growing larger and larger with each exhalation. When you feel totally surrounded by this imaginary bubble, mentally fill it with your favorite color, so the bubble becomes more visible. You can make it change color several times, if you wish. Each time you make the bubble change color, allow yourself to experience the sensations that the particular color provides.

When you are ready to meet your guardian angel, make the bubble return to your favorite color, and then ask your guardian angel to join you. Your special angel will appear inside the bubble. You may see him in your mind's eye, or you may experience him simply as a sense of knowing that he is present with you.

Once you sense his presence, start a conversation with your guardian angel. You will probably start by thanking him for helping you progress through life. If you have a special need for your guardian angel because of a particular situation in your life, discuss that with your angel. You can discuss anything at all.

After you've gone over everything you had in mind, thank your guardian angel for coming to your aid, and say goodbye. Visualize the bubble of air around you and see it gradually dissipating until it completely disappears. Take three more slow, deep breaths and open your eyes.

Invocation Four

You will need a candle and a table to place it on for this invocation. As you will have your eyes closed for part of the invocation, make sure the candle is secure before you start. I usually use a white candle for invocations of this sort, but you can use any color you wish as long as it is pleasing to you.

Light the candle, and sit down about six feet away from it. When you look straight ahead, the candle flame should be at eye level. Make yourself as comfortable as possible.

Gaze at the flame and think about your need to contact your guardian angel. After a minute or two, your eyes will start feeling heavy. Let them close when this occurs. Take a slow, deep breath and ask your guardian angel to contact you. Wait for about a minute to see if your guardian angel starts putting thoughts in your mind. Begin communicating with your guardian angel if he makes contact with you.

If he does not make contact, remain sitting quietly with your eyes closed, and talk about your need and desire to contact your guardian angel. Thank him for what he has done for you in the past and say how much you are looking forward to establishing an even closer bond with him in the future. Pause for another minute to see if he wants to respond. Obviously, if he does start talking, engage him in conversation. If not, thank him again, and tell him you'll try again, and that you will keep on trying until he does contact you.

Take a slow, deep breath, and open your eyes. Stand up and pick up the candle. Hold it high in front of you. Say "thank you" out loud, and finish the invocation by snuffing out the candle.

~

These are my favorite invocations for contacting a guardian angel. Over the years, my students and I have experimented with many different rituals and invocations, and these are the ones that have proved most effective. I like the first invocation best but use all of them at different times. Experiment for yourself to see which invocation you like best. Continue performing the invocation at least once a week until you have established regular communication with your guardian angel.

Bibliography

Adler, Mortimer. *The Angels and Us*. New York: Macmillan and Company, 1982.

Agrippa, Henry Cornelius. *Fourth Book of Occult Philosophy*. London: Askin Publishers, 1978. (Includes: *Of Occult Magical Ceremonies* by Agrippa; *Heptameron or Magical Elements* by Peter de Abano; *Of the Nature of Spirits* by Georg Villinganus; *Arbatel of Magick*; *Of Geomancy* by Agrippa; *Of Astronomical Geomancy* by Gerard Cremonensis.)

———. *Three Books of Occult Philosophy*. Ed. and annotated by Donald Tyson. St. Paul, MN: Llewellyn Publications, 1993. (originally published in Antwerp in 1531.)

Aquinas, St. Thomas. *Summa Theologiae*. 5 vols. Cambridge, England: Cambridge University Press, 2006. (Many versions available.)

Ashton, John, and Tom Whyte. *The Quest for Paradise: Visions of Heaven and Eternity in the World's Myths and Religions*. London: New Burlington Books, 2001.

Barrett, Francis. *The Magus*. Wellingborough, UK: The Aquarian Press, 1989. Originally published in 1801.

Blavatsky, H. P. *The Secret Doctrine*. Volume IV. Adyar, India: Theosophical Publishing House, Adyar Edition, 1922.

Bonaventure. *The Soul's Journey into God; The Tree of Life; The Life of St. Francis*. Trans. and ed. Ewart Cousins. Mahwah, NJ: Paulist Press, 1978.

Briggs, Constance Victoria. *The Encyclopedia of God.* Charlottesville, NC: Hampton Roads Publishing Company, 2003.

Calmet, Augustin. *The Phantom World.* Ware, UK: Wordsworth Editions Limited, 2001. (Originally published in Paris, 1746.)

Charles, R. H., ed. and trans. *The Book of Enoch (Enoch I).* Oxford, UK: The Clarendon Press, 1912.

———, ed. and trans. *The Book of Jubilees.* London: Society for Promoting Christian Knowledge, 1927.

———, ed. and trans. *The Syriac Apocalypse of Baruch (Baruch II).* London: Society for Promoting Christian Knowledge, 1918.

Charlesworth, James H., ed. *The Old Testament Pseudepigrapha.* 2 vols. New York: Doubleday and Company, 1985.

Chase, Steven. *Angelic Spirituality: Medieval Perspectives on the Ways of Angels.* Mahwah, NJ: Paulist Press, 2002.

Cicero, Chic, and Sandra Tabatha Cicero. *Tarot Talismans: Invoke the Angels of the Tarot.* Woodbury, MN: Llewellyn Publications, 2006.

Colet, John. *Two Treatises on the Hierarchies of Dionysius.* London: G. Bell & Sons, 1869.

Connolly, David. *In Search of Angels: A Celestial Sourcebook for Beginning Your Journey.* New York: Perigee Books, 1993.

Cruz, John Carroll. *Angels and Devils.* Rockford, IL: Tan Books and Publishers, 1999.

Davidson, Gustav. *A Dictionary of Angels.* New York: The Free Press, 1967.

Dennis, Rabbi Geoffrey W. *The Encyclopedia of Jewish Myth, Magic and Mysticism.* Woodbury, MN: Llewellyn Publications, 2007.

Deutsch, Nathaniel. *The Gnostic Imagination: Gnosticism, Mandaeism, and Merkabah Mysticism.* Leiden, Netherlands: E. J. Brill, 1995.

Dickason, C. Fred. *Angels, Elect and Evil.* Chicago: Moody Press, 1975.

Duff, Archibald. *The First and Second Books of Esdras.* London: J. M. Dent & Company, 1903.

Eleazer of Worms (credited to). *The Book of the Angel Raziel (Sepher Raziel)*. York Beach, ME: Samuel Weiser, 1978.

Field, M. J. *Angels and Ministers of Grace*. London: Longman Group Limited, 1971.

Garfield, Laeh Maggie and Jack Grant. *Angels and Companions in Spirit*. Berkeley, CA: Celestial Arts Publishing, 1984.

Ginzberg, Louis. *Legends of the Jews*. Trans. Henrietta Szold and Paul Radin. Philadelphia, PA: The Jewish Publication Society, 2003. (Originally published in seven volumes between 1909 and 1938.)

Giovetti, Paola. *Angels: The Role of Celestial Guardians and Beings of Light*. York Beach, ME: Samuel Weiser, 1993.

Godwin, Malcolm. *Angels: An Endangered Species*. New York: Simon and Schuster, 1990.

Graham, Billy. *Angels: God's Secret Agents*. New York: Pocket Books, 1975.

Hall, Manley P. *The Blessed Angels*. Los Angeles: The Philosophical Research Society, 1980.

Harkness, Deborah E. *John Dee's Conversations with Angels*. Cambridge, UK: Cambridge University Press, 1999.

Heywood, Thomas. *The Hierarchy of the Blessed Angels*. London: Adam Islip, 1635.

Hodson, Geoffrey. *The Brotherhood of Angels and Men*. Wheaton, IL: The Theosophical Publishing House, 1982. (Originally published in 1927.)

———. *The Kingdom of the Gods*. Adyar, India: The Theosophical Publishing House, 1952.

Humann, Harvey. *The Many Faces of Angels*. Marina del Rey, CA: DeVorss & Company, 1986.

Jackson, Nigel and Michael Howard. *The Pillars of Tubal-Cain*. Chieveley, UK: Capall Bann Publishing, 2000.

Jovanovic, Pierre. *An Inquiry into the Existence of Guardian Angels*. New York: M. Evans and Company, 1995.

Keck, David. *Angels and Angelology in the Middle Ages*. Oxford, UK: Oxford University Press, 1998.

Langton, Edward. *Good and Evil Spirits*. London: Society for Promoting Christian Knowledge, 1942.

Layton, Bentley, trans. *The Gnostic Scriptures*. New York: Doubleday & Company, 1987.

MacGregor, Geddes. *Angels: Ministers of Grace*. New York: Paragon House, 1988.

Margolies, Rabbi Morris B. *A Gathering of Angels*. New York: Ballantine Books, 1994.

Mathers, S. L. MacGregor, ed. *The Greater Key of Solomon*. Chicago: The de Laurence Company, 1914.

Mathers, S. L. MacGregor. *The Kabbalah Unveiled*. London: George Redway, 1887.

Maxwell-Stuart, P. G. *Wizards: A History*. Stroud, UK: Tempus Publishing Limited, 2004.

McDannell, Colleen, and Bernhard Lang. *Heaven: A History*. New Haven, CT: Yale University Press, 1988.

Metzger, Bruce M., ed. *The Oxford Annotated Apocrypha*. New York: Oxford University Press, 1965.

Moolenburgh, Hans. *A Handbook of Angels*. Saffron Walden, UK: C. W. Daniel Company Limited, 1984.

Muhammad, Shaykh, and Hisham Kabbani. *Angels Unveiled: A Sufi Perspective*. Chicago: KAZI Publications, 1995.

Peterson, Joseph, ed. *The Lesser Key of Solomon: Lemegeton Clavicula Salomonis*. York Beach, ME: Red Wheel/Weiser, 2001.

Pseudo-Dionysius. *The Complete Works*. Trans. Colm Luibheid. New York: Paulist Press, 1987.

Richards, Larry. *Every Good and Evil Angel in the Bible.* Nashville, TN: Thomas Nelson Publishers, 1998.

Ronner, John. *Know Your Angels.* Murfreesboro, TN: Mamre Press, 1993.

Ronner, John, with Fran Gangloff, Sr. *The Angel Calendar Book.* Murfreesboro, TN: Mamre Press, 2000.

Russell, Jeffrey Burton. *A History of Heaven: The Singing Silence.* Princeton, NJ: Princeton University Press, 1997.

———. *Paradise Mislaid: How We Lost Heaven—and How We Can Regain It.* New York: Oxford University Press, 2006.

Schueler, Gerald, and Betty Schueler. *The Angel's Message to Humanity.* St. Paul, MN: Llewellyn Publications, 1996.

Skinner, Stephen, and David Rankine. *The Goetia of Dr Rudd.* London: Golden Hoard Press, 2007.

———. *Practical Angel Magic of Dr. John Dee's Enochian Tables.* London: Golden Hoard Press, 2004.

———. *Summoning the Solomonic Archangels & Demon Princes.* London: Golden Hoard Press, 2005.

Spence, Lewis. *The Encyclopedia of the Occult.* London: Bracken Books, 1994.

Sperling, Harry, and Maurice Simon, trans. *The Zohar.* 5 vols. London: The Soncino Press, 1956.

Steiner, Rudolf. *The Archangel Michael: His Mission and Ours.* Great Barrington, MA: Anthroposophic Press, 1994.

Swedenborg, Emmanuel. *Heaven and Hell.* New York: Swedenborg Foundation, 1990.

Trachtenberg, Joshua. *Jewish Magic and Superstition.* New York: Behrman's Jewish Book House, 1939.

Tyson, Donald. *Enochian Magic for Beginners.* St. Paul, MN: Llewellyn Publications, 1997.

Webster, Richard. *Communicating with the Archangel Gabriel for Inspiration and Reconciliation*. St. Paul, MN: Llewellyn Publications, 2005.

———. *Communicating with the Archangel Michael for Guidance and Protection*. St. Paul, MN: Llewellyn Publications, 2004.

———. *Communicating with the Archangel Raphael for Healing and Creativity*. St. Paul, MN: Llewellyn Publications, 2005.

———. *Communicating with the Archangel Uriel for Transformation and Tranquility*. Woodbury, MN: Llewellyn Publications, 2005.

———. *Praying with Angels*. Woodbury, MN: Llewellyn Publications, 2007.

———. *Spirit Guides and Angel Guardians*. St. Paul, MN: Llewellyn Publications, 1998.

Internet Sources

Anon. *Arbatel of Magic*. 1575. http://www.esotericarchives.com/solomon/arbatel.htm

———. *Lemegeton Clavicula Salomonis*. "The Lesser Key of Solomon." 17th century. http://www.esotericarchives.com/solomon/lemegeton.htm

———. *Liber Juratus* or *The Sworn Book of Honorius*. 13th century. http://www.esotericarchives.com/juratus/juratus.htm

Charles, R. H., trans. 1906. *Book of Enoch, The*. http://www.ancienttexts.org/library/ethiopian/enoch/index.html

Conybeare, F. C., trans. 1898. *The Testament of Solomon*. 1st to 3rd century. http://www.esotericarchives.com/solomon/testamen.htm

de Abano, Peter. *Heptameron* or *Magical Elements*. Trans. Robert Turner, 1655. http://www.esotericarchives.com/solomon/heptamer.htm

Mead, G. R. S., trans. 1921. *Pistis Sophia*. http://www.sacred-texts.com/chr/ps/index.htm

Index